I0816188

The most important project for a design studio is the design of the practice itself.

FOUNDATIONS

CONTENTS

PROPOSITIONS

FOUNDATIONS

GROUND WORK

The most important project for a design studio is the design of the practice itself. A studio's point of view is often first expressed by feelings and hopes but, if cultivated, grows into values and tactics. Crafting the studio environment and cultivating a kinship around this point of view with collaborators, clients, consultants, community members, and contractors is essential for a studio to be productive and have a healthy impact. The ecology of a design studio is not fixed. It is an open, iterative work, matured over time through many projects and with many people. The studio's early critiques begin to establish the approach and territory of work and pose the questions that are asked of every project. The studio environment and relationships create the space for the work to develop. With discipline, a studio evolves and shapes the character, performance, and value of the work over time.

Design encompasses life in all its complexities and contingencies. Planning and design are the only activities that can improve the social and environmental health of our communities. Any professional can engage planning and design thinking in their work, but designers are trained for this challenge. Design methodologies include imagining a future and defining the systematic steps to achieve that future. Architectural projects are local and sited in a specific place and community. To have meaningful impact, architecture must be grounded in the place of practice, in its soil, weather, economy, history, and social context. To be productive, a studio must be aware of the cultural history and limitations of architecture and search for critiques and improvements that can help make a socially and environmentally healthy condition.

The first and earliest proposition for our studio was a belief that all architecture is public work. This immediately relocated the site of the design work and dissolved the artificial separation between the subject and object. Ego is displaced with empathy. Form is neither the thing nor its perception; it is the living transactional space between these two artificial poles. We became focused on the character and value of this space and the consequences of the work in public life. This first proposition led to the others, starting with the character and quality of experience (the physical presence and psychological posture facilitated in the work), the opportunities to re-think authority (the politic in form), the consideration of the work as leverage to amplify our investments beyond design and construction, the expansion of the practice to be responsible for the quality of the life of the building beyond its making, and the exploration of the didactic value of sites/buildings to be open opportunities for inquiry. Later, we deepened our inquiry to consider architecture as a scaffold or even a more intentional instrument that can be productively critical, to amplify the quality of phenomena, and build a kind of open resonance in experience. We considered the making of the work as an integrated effort—an orchestration of place, people, material, needs, and desires—to create a critical and cultural artifact, one that connects to the past, is present, and looks forward to being better, all leading us back to the beginning to interrogate public work as embodied living witness.

From the beginning, we understood that the integrity of the work depended on the integrity of the practice—the daily decisions we would make to define the world we create and maintain. We began the practice by interrogating everything we did in the work—in the make-up of the studio, in the business, and in our relationship as architects with collaborators, clients, consultants, community members, and contractors. While the propositions set out the territory of work, the daily tactics guided our specific actions to achieve the values set out by our early feelings and hopes. These tactics became foundations for practice. Over time, we kept a list. Each foundation grew out of the daily work to strive for a consequential practice. Some of the foundations are simple, some are reminders of how we should behave, some are more philosophical, and some grew out of either failures or successes. They include everything from design goals and cautions on business operations to reminders to get away from it all and take time off and travel. The list has grown into 53 foundations for daily practice. This is not a complete list, nor are the foundations fixed. We are a studio striving to learn and do better together. They serve as guides and reminders to act with care and integrity each day. As new team members join the studio, the list, now attached to all offers of employment, has been instrumental in expanding the culture of the studio and inviting new voices into the conversation.

At Duvall Decker, we understand that meaningful work requires more than service, ego, profit, or simple function. We are most interested in the consequences of a work in its context. We believe that architectural interventions in any community or landscape can be therapeutic and didactic. They reflect who we are and, through our interaction over time, teach us who we might become. This viewpoint identifies added value beyond simple service or aesthetic merit. Since many project parameters are defined before architects are engaged, our approach often requires re-defining the problem. Many of the foundations grew out of the desire to foster meaningful work and facilitate healthy outcomes in each project.

We knew our initial proposition for the design of a business was challenging. We were naive in some ways, and in other ways, we were not. We knew we wanted to design a business that was sustainable, but we did not want to confuse profit or spectacle with public value. This position ran headstrong against the conventional expectations to be either a typical service-labor-based architecture firm or a special boutique design firm serving an elite clientele. We wanted the work to elevate public good. We knew that design excellence required design time. We wanted to practice with a high degree of professional integrity, be an active partner during construction, teach craft, and make an educational environment for young architects. We knew that a work of quality requires many diverse voices. We wanted a studio of collaborators who respect and learn from each other. We sought to pay the highest wages we could, offer profit sharing, health care, and a 401k program, and we wanted to maintain a work environment that was healthy, family supportive, and joyful. Additionally, and remarkably, we had no subsidy or safety net. One of us, Roy, had left his tenured teaching position at Mississippi State University and the other, Anne Marie, her full-time position in another firm. Neither of us had connections or family in the area nor financial savings or endowments. This was from the very start a design problem, as important as the approach to the work.

We believe architecture matters. It is a reflection of both place and culture and, in turn, a teacher. We feel responsible to both serve and lead, to solve problems, and be productively critical. We are in a place where there is an abundance of social, environmental, and economic problems. We have limited resources, a challenging climate, and poor soils. There are harsh challenges to human dignity and inspiring individuals who fight for equity and justice and find beauty in this place every day. We are in a position to make a difference through an architectural practice that searches for public good by making interventions that are healthy, equitable, and durable in material and memory.

Duvall Decker was formed, in part, as an educational experiment. With our limited resources, could we start and sustain a firm in a place of great need, create an environment of teaching and learning, and create work with public value? In a way, we offer this book as a status report on our experiment.

Nine (9) Propositions and fifty-three (53) Foundations are shared herein. Each foundation additionally includes a supportive commentary. Some of the commentaries explore our attempts to live up to these proposals when we found them "hard to hold" (a phrase we use often about the difficulty of holding principles), and we were challenged to compromise. Others chronicle successes, failures, lessons learned, inspirations, and some hopeful examples in the projects. As we look back over the text, the years, the work, the propositions, and foundations, it occurs to us how important both optimism, measured by skepticism and ambition, challenged by humility, are in the designs and the day-to-day work of the studio. Both the foundations and propositions are presented as works in progress. These are lists that chronicle our thinking and doing over twenty-five (25) years. For us, there is no separation between theory and practice. This collection of foundations and propositions captures an approach to the work and way of being an architect. Practicing architecture is a privilege with public responsibilities. This is one studio's search for public good.

Anne Marie Duvall Decker, FAIA
Roy T. Decker, FAIA

01

ENIGMA

Making useful and engaging architecture is not about, or limited to, the logic of problem-solving or service. Engaging form is enigmatic, elusive, open, and hard to know fully. Only the architect who makes an enigma of the solution is involved in making art.

So much of contemporary experience tells us (with packaged, efficient concept communication) what to do or think, what group to belong to, what is fashionable, what to buy, and even what is truth. This is the authority of language as explanation and instruction. These explanations and instructions have many motives—some benevolent, some benign, some manipulative, and some exploitative. The speed and efficiency of concept communication can suppress other modes of experience. To the degree we acquiesce as a society, we risk forfeiting opportunities for individual inquiry.

When architectural forms are dominated by content communication, simplistic typologies, or functional structures, (whether useful or expressive), experience is narrowed. Inquiry is suppressed, and the discernment of broader, formal, and environmental qualities is limited. When we read concepts embedded in architectural projects, witness is thinned to these concepts. Pre-verbal, full-bodied experience can remain distant, or worse, bypassed altogether.

One of our earliest hopes for the work of the practice was to awaken witness (the interactive space of transaction between perception and things), to foster pre-verbal, full-bodied qualitative inquiry, and to ground the work in its place—in the soil, light, weather, economy, and culture. Architecture is experienced over time. We experience buildings like the Kimball Art Museum, by Louis Kahn, that seem alive; character, dimensions, textures, colors, and art change with the time of day and the weather. As clouds pass over the Kimball galleries, the space darkens and seems to breathe in. With the brightness of the returning sunlight, the space then breathes out. The dimensions and character of the space are in motion. Witness is opened to the full-bodied experience of the moment—in the environment, in the building, and with the art. This quality of aliveness presents an opportunity to see form as neither the object nor the subject but the space between, elusive and open. We work for this kind of elusive space.

02

ART

History tells our story. Science explores how things work. Philosophy interrogates our beliefs. Art is the only human discipline that has the power to ask who we might become and how we might be better. When we see art as a creative search for public good, it ceases to be a personal aesthetic conceit and has the power to enhance cultural and environmental quality.

The art of the work for us has always been the search for public value in witness. The work of an artist who speculates on their world can be celebratory, critical, educational, therapeutic, or a combination of some or all of these. In the search for public good in architecture, we listen and research, wonder how things work, and ponder our beliefs through the design process. It is perhaps more important than ever to see architecture not as an aesthetic or formal endeavor alone, but as the art of critical and productive work, challenging and offering an alternative to the automatic economic, functional, or stylistic typologies that perpetuate outworn, unjust, and unhealthy traditions.

The design of the Cooperwood Senior Living complex was, from the start, an artistic search for a more engaging and lively home for the elderly. We pursued a critical re-making of the institutional typology by prioritizing natural light, air, proportion, color, shape, and pattern along with function. The design attempts to bring dignity to this new and expanding living typology. The design accepts that there are two scales to embrace and integrate—the intimate scale of each resident's home and the community scale of the common spaces. Experience with aging parents implored developing the simple livability of the units as well as reconsidering the traditional four-square room where residents, depending upon their health, may spend many hours of the day and night. The simple addition of splayed exterior walls, larger-than-normal windows, and sunshades animate the interior with slightly different and expansive views of the landscape and bring ever-changing colors of natural light deep into the spaces without glare. The form and siting of the building with its faceted pattern of exterior walls at play in the sunlight build a dynamic concurrence among several contingent formal strategies. The complex feels alive with both a familiar and unfamiliar presence which we consider an example of uncanny form.

Within four months of opening, the complex was nearly fully occupied. Residents and staff members, citing the quality of the design, spaces, and environment, came from other assisted living projects to live and work at Cooperwood.

03

ENGAGEMENT

Engaging buildings entangle us in a world of difference and description. Explanation and its forces of simplification are necessarily pushed to the background.

When architectural designs are primarily based on a program or other simplistic formal strategies, they telegraph an explanation of their makeup into our experience. We are all accustomed to "reading" the limited intentions of these ubiquitous buildings that instruct our behavior and condition our responses. Experience is thinned to visual consumption followed quickly by conceptual recognition.

Engaging form challenges us to consider qualities and relations. Witness opens to inquiry and engenders us to discern differences and attempt descriptions. Qualitative strategies can make connections to the environment and the culture of a place and challenge simplistic language structures to open form to broader, slower inquiry. Whether in its shaping, its structure, or its connections to an aliveness in the environment, multiple dimensions of witness can open the possibility to delay knowing. Think of Cézanne's still-life compositional distortions or Sean Scully's challenges to surface and measure and how they invite us to consider differences. When form is crafted to be alive in its environment, it can be different from visit to visit and open the need for comparison and reconsideration in memory. When form is familiar and unfamiliar at the same time, it offers an uncanny disturbance in experience that is awakening. Each example makes space for lived experience to promote our discernment of the qualities and differences that we come to know as character and presence.

The Mississippi Library Commission was an early effort to test this thesis. The variegated precast surface of the building thickens with the highlights and shadows of direct sun and flattens when a cloud diffuses the sun's light. The sixty-foot-wide footprint of the north wing of the building and the configuration of its section allows east and west light to course equally into the interior, characterizing the space with the honey-colored glow of the morning and the redder glow of the afternoon. The space of the reading room, illuminated by the northern sky, seems to contract and expand with the changing brightness and passing clouds of the day. The non-traditional and indirect planning continually offers spaces to pause with inner horizons to the spaces beyond and invitations to explore. Each of these strategies and qualities attempts to slow knowing and open opportunities for engagement.

04

CRITICAL PRACTICE

Practice critically. Challenge the simplistic, nominal, and conceptual biases common in our time. Avoid borrowed culture and question the value of precedents. Search for work that springs from the soil, weather, economy, craft, and social context of a place. Create surprise, joy, wonder, and desire. Promote social, economic, and environmental health. Resist the structures of authority and instruction that frame social divisions and constrain the power of diversity. Empower the possibilities of individual growth.

There has been much written about what constitutes a critical practice. Conceptual, stylistic, historical, technical, or performance concerns are common, but social, political, and economic issues are often neglected. For Duvall Decker, a critical practice has a hopeful mission at its core. We see the potential for an architectural practice and its work, quietly, to be educational and therapeutic. We see opportunities for architects to facilitate mature conversations about what is public good, and to help find ways that we can be better, together. Every meeting, presentation, lecture, and conversation offers opportunities to describe how the built environment can promote social and environmental health. We believe that culture grows from the local and finds transformative value in working from a specific place, in its soil, weather, economy, history, and social context. We see the value of working in our time and looking forward. We suffer the harm done when architects appeal to taste and reduce architecture to a consumer artifact. Resisting traditional structures of authority in form opens the possibility for plural social/political spaces. Opening the center, elevating the in-between, challenging the simplistic, and avoiding the singular empower those traditionally pushed to the margins. We see this as part of a search for a more mature, diverse society.

We are indebted to Kenneth Frampton and his article "Towards a Critical Regionalism" where he proposes that the Enlightenment myth of progress with its blind faith in technology, entertainment, and consumerism, is as empty as nostalgic historicism.[1] He advocates for a redressing of the visual, "scenographic" universality of modern form with a return to local "tactile experience." On this foundation, Duvall Decker's search for critical form attempts to look deeper into the conditions that make up a place, understanding its social, economic, historical, and political circumstances. We are in Mississippi working where the needs are greatest. We identify circumstances that are unhealthy or unjust, that limit opportunity or individual growth, and we intervene with leadership by promoting inquiry, safety, social equity, and environmental health. We see this critical grounding of the work as finding a therapeutic resonance with the places where we practice.

CAMP
SHELBY

ITERATION

05

Build a practice of repetition and research. Test ideas and materials over many projects. Do not simply repeat a detail. Increase our understanding of its make-up and performance. Re-make the detail with more refined knowledge. Take the time required to make drawings, models, and mock-ups to raise questions that improve design quality and performance.

Architectural practice as a service is too often measured by hours and not by the value created. Market-based fees account for the work required to produce a design, construction documents, and the oversight of construction, but not much more. The fees measured by this simplistic formula allow limited time for design investigations or research to achieve excellence.

We know that design excellence requires time, questioning, experimentation, failure, and above all, criticism and iteration. Design excellence is a "patient search," not a rush to a product. The end is in sight but not clear. Through research, site investigations, historic and demographic research, community engagement, models, and drawings, we pursue incremental growth toward a proposal of meaning and quality.

Early in our practice, we realized that we had to buy design time not with more or higher fees (although we were always trying to increase our fees to account for the true value of the work), but with efficiency and iteration. Out of this realization, we developed checklists to standardize the routine and avoid simple mistakes. We focused on deep understanding and limited our palette to a small group of materials and products. We built our knowledge and skill in one project and re-invested the value created in the next one, continuing our research and deepening our understanding with each iteration. As we have designed more complicated projects, we have expanded our tactics and proposals but have continued this discipline. When we add to the palette, it is only with a combination of need and skepticism. We seek a specific quality and utilize a new material that offers it, but we interrogate the material's properties and performance with doubt. With each project, we hone our checklists, templates, material research, and examples, and invest that time saved and deep understanding into better buildings. We buy design and research time with disciplined efficiency.

06

ETHIC

Produce complete and effective construction drawings and specifications that clearly describe the requirements of construction, communicate an ethic of quality and craft, and promote fairness in the process.

The ethic of quality—the principles and requirements for a project—grows from the design process. The translation of design quality into construction documents is like translating an English text into Arabic. The language of construction is entirely different from the language that describes the character and quality of spatial use and experience. The ethic can get lost in translation.

Construction documents have several purposes. First, they are bid documents in which many subcontractors discern their scope of work from the assembly to provide their costs and labor estimates. Second, they are contract documents that form the base of an agreement for construction. Third, they are the description of the building, its systems, materials, and performance. We are good students of how our construction documents are understood and utilized, and we work to continually improve their effectiveness. We learn from our failures and successes. We have developed systematic strategies to clearly translate design quality into effective construction documents to serve all three of the purposes. Many contractors and subcontractors adopt the ethic of quality and become essential partners in achieving design excellence. Some contractors resist the quality standards articulated in the documents. In those cases, the documents become enforcement tools. In either case, we support the work with an ethic of quality and, over the years, have heard from all types of contractors and subcontractors that our documents are clear and detailed and our construction administration processes are tough but also fair.

Public Work

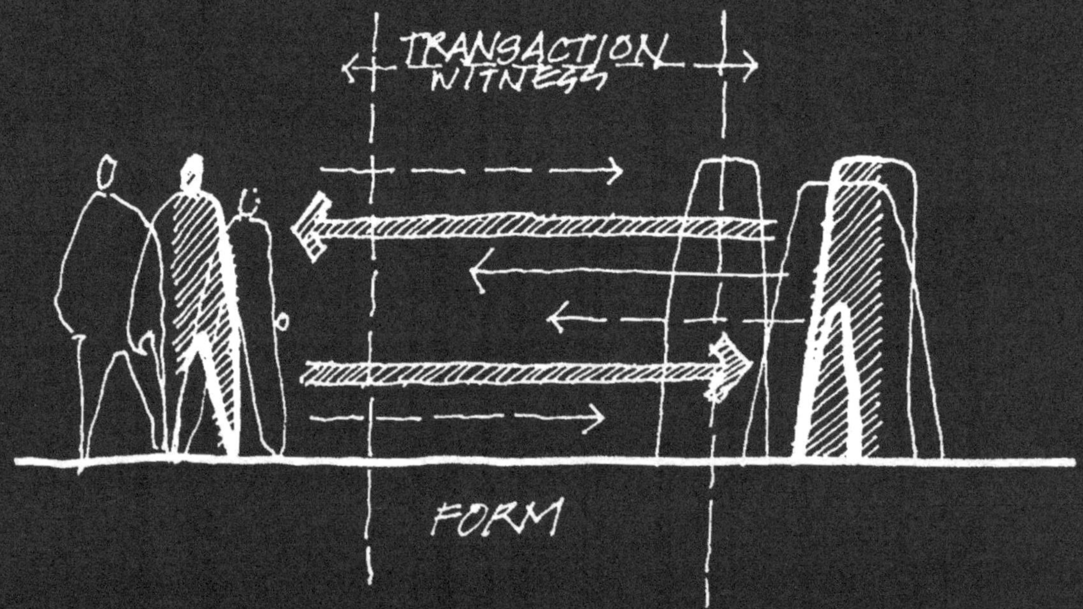

Form is neither the object nor the perception of the object. It is the field of transaction between and amongst us and things. The transactions are valuable when they can be critical, educational, equitable, healthy, and therapeutic—when they foster hope to speculate upon who we might become. This is the art of the work. Art is the only discipline that has the power to speculate upon who we might become.

We believe architecture is more than a functional shelter. While architects are responsible for a program, budget, and schedule, these are the technical rudiments of building and little more. Architects must create objects and space conceived to foster transactions of public value. Each project can be engaged in its place, its history, and culture and amplify the best that it can be. Projects can be entangled in the phenomena of their environment, be ecologically responsible, and invite inquiry. They can be empathetic and find resonance with our shared experiences while challenging us all to be equitable and just.

With each new or renovated building, each newly developed site, park, street, school, library, home, or business, a community is changed. The changes bring with them consequences in the lives of those who encounter them—from homeowners to citizens in public space. With every project, we ask ourselves, "What is the public value of each intervention? How can the constructed environment be critical, educational, and perhaps, therapeutic for a place and its inhabitants?" We use these questions to help push us beyond the confines of ego, appearance, taste, construction, energy performance, and use.

07

IDEAS

Never proceed without an idea. Architectural ideas are larger and more encompassing than the program or site. They entangle us first in questions of nature and culture, then gravity, light, materials, labor, and use. A formal idea attempts to make the ideal present in the real, the abstract in the concrete. Ideas reduce the infinite possibilities to allow focus. Ideas, when large and compelling enough, envelope the owner, staff, community, and contractor. They become the mission of the work that helps carry all through the tedious and complicated work to make any project real.

Architectural ideas—when grounded in the specifics of a place, land, light, climate, culture, and lives of everyday witnesses—are alive and have public value. John Dewey, in *Experience and Nature*, reminds us that things do not have relationships; they have relations.[2] This means that each intervention is alive in time, in experience, and is not defined by limited explanations. Formal concepts and orders, when imposed as an underlying reason for form, are an architect's conceit which often misses the opportunity to connect form to place in meaningful ways.

The culture of a place is always local in that the collective sense of citizens who live and work together piles up qualities and figures into a kind of abstraction, a kind of dream of a place where memory, presence, and anticipation unite. As new buildings/sites are added, they intervene in this dream space and fundamentally change the experience of everyone in the community. For us, the site of form is in the living space of the work outside its making—in the community and connected to the collective dream of a place. We believe that for a work to be critical, therapeutic, and productive, it must also be subversive and deny the propensity in our culture to assemble known concepts, historical facsimiles, commercialized typologies, and cliches. We work to make fields of experience, sited in the space between, that are elusive and awaken and expand a subject's perceptual apparatus. We search for architectural ideas that are public and strive for interventions that are enigmatic.

08

CARVED VALUE

Create therapeutic figures/spaces that appeal to pre-verbal qualities of experience. Develop formal strategies, ideas, materials, systems, and products to form figures of integrity that open inquiry. Overcome the fragmentary, additive reality of design and construction. Avoid modeled assembly and additive work (forms, products, and ideas) that are easily co-opted by language.

In *The Image in Form,* Adrian Stokes describes a model of form that was grounded in formative experience which presented a kind of otherness or independent integrity.[3] He described this work as exhibiting a psycho-spatial exposure position formed with smooth internal transitions, embodied internal energy, and formal cohesion. These works exhibited carved value which can be both a provocation and an invitation in form that challenges witness. For Stokes, encounters with a work that exhibits carved value can open inquiry and the possibility of therapeutic growth. By contrast, a modeled work is characterized as a fragmented collection of parts with internal differentiation, exposed connections, and sometimes, an arbitrary ordering device to hold a composition together. Witness of modeled form can be enveloping; the spectator becomes a fragment among fragments in a possibly pleasurable but unproductive assemblage in experience.

Stokes recognized that we live in a fragmented world and often manage experience additively. However, he challenged artists to seek form that could achieve carved value, even with additive means of construction. In our search for examples in art, we have found carved value in works of art created through additive means. In sculptures by David Smith, the assemblage of parts is held together by a cohesion of common energy. In Kurt Schwitters's collages, the phenomenally transparent positioning of disparate components binds parts into an open ensemble. In Cezanne's paintings, the perspectival adjustments of distributed figures form a tension in witness, and a textural applied color palette bridges differences to make both a scene and a surface hold together.

Experiments to achieve carved form in the work can be found in the composite shape transformations in the Mississippi Library Commission, the overlapped interior spaces experienced as pause and move plans in multiple projects, and the distributed figures between sister components in the Clarksdale Coahoma Higher Education Center and the Springdale Municipal Complex.

09

PRAGMATIC VALUE

Ideas are valuable when they produce productive consequences. We are pragmatic architects. We search for meaningful form through ideas and material that can be manifested and verified in witness.

We believe that the consequences of the work matter in the community and in the lives of those who encounter the places made. For us, ideas are not remote or superfluously applied to the work. They are only valuable if they are productive in the lived space of the project. This stance challenges us to verify design proposals. We search for ideas that are productive, or as the pragmatists say, have "cash value" and are useful. We see the possibilities for architecture and design planning to intervene in this lived space in active and productive ways.

We rely on our direct experience with projects, clients, communities, materials, and contractors and trades in construction as sources of knowledge. We support our experiments with research. We are dedicated students of each place and site where we work. We listen and learn from community members, clients, and craftsmen. We have a limited palette of materials we use and reuse, each time learning more of their properties and qualities.

Through our facility maintenance work, we have learned countless direct and valuable lessons on the material and operational consequences of the work. One of the first buildings we cared for was one we designed, the Mississippi Library Commission. During design, we made many decisions based on how to harden the infrastructure to make a more durable long-term building. Many of these decisions were validated as we maintained and cared for the building. One lesson involved the sealant used for the precast concrete panel joints. After ten years, the sealant began to fail. We discovered that the issue was due to bats, who had begun roosting in the cavity place. We learned about the limitations of sealant in southern sun and how to remove bats from inside the walls at the top of a three-story building.

10

ECONOMY

Quality requires economy. Do more with less.

We often work with limited resources and in situations where there are insufficient funds for maintenance. We have learned to maximize the long-term durability of a project while allowing for change. In design, we imagine the life cycle of the project and its components, the use of the building over time, and its needed flexibility. A building's infrastructure, such as foundations, structure, enclosure, and major circulation routes, often must last for generations. Mechanical systems have an approximate 25-year life. Communication and data systems have a shorter five-year life. Individual functions can often change even before the building is complete. We work to build a distinction between what is infrastructure and what is transitory. We strive to make the infrastructure limited, legible, efficient, accessible, and durable. We invest in what will last and work to facilitate easy access for system maintenance, future technology upgrades, and changes in use.

Needs often exceed the initial funds available for public projects. Working through many public design-bid-build processes, we have learned how to get the most out of the project funding, how to be economical, preserve an owner's priorities, and achieve design excellence. The first and most economical question to ask is, "Can we renovate an existing building instead of demolishing and rebuilding?" Renovation is both more economical and more environmentally responsible. For the Dumas Hall project at Alcorn State University, saving the original concrete structural frame netted a nearly one-million-dollar credit for the project and allowed a more durable, useful, and valuable academic building to return to campus.

The second strategy is to focus resources on the design and construction of the infrastructure. Capitalize first on the design elements that are free using proportion, color, and light with simple economical materials to establish the character and quality of the design proposal. We often see other architects and projects, pressured by owners or driven by taste and appearance, rush to add historical details, stripes, and other embellishments before the basic design quality is established. Often, the result is that embellishments appear as an apology for the lack of basic design quality. Last, we limit finishes and overlays. Unless steel needs fire protection, it is more durable on its own than with a column cover. A concrete block wall, if it is carefully laid, is more durable than a furred-painted gypsum board wall. Ground face can be a rich natural surface and pays for itself the first time you do not have to re-paint.

During the design process, resources are measured against the design opportunities at every step. We work with limited resources in a state that is used to "making do." Our questions are always focused on how to "do more with less."

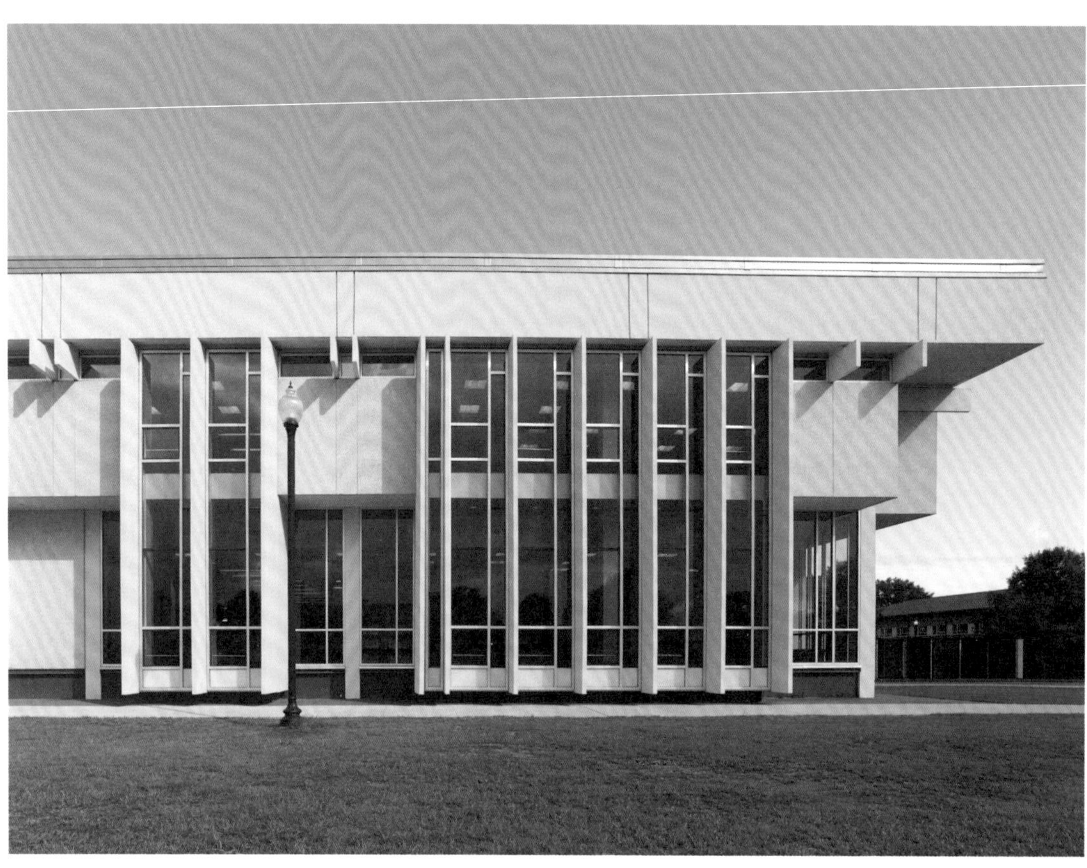

11

RESPONSIBILITY

Practice with integrity and character. Be a leader, be responsible, and be fair to both client and contractor. Be a leader in the process. Work for social, economic, and environmental health. That is our expertise. To maintain this authority, we must be students of the communities where we work, know the costs, know the contractual relationships, and have good design and construction documents. We take responsibility for our leadership.

We believe architecture is more than shelter for a group of functions, more than status for an individual or institution, and more than spectacle for entertainment. While architects are responsible for a client's program, budget, and schedule, these are merely the technical rudiments of building. If a work is to be architecture, it should foster critical, educational, or therapeutic public experiences. It should strive to be inspirational, achieve comprehensive performance, help make a healthier society and environment, and be a meaningful contribution to its community's story.

Design is more than problem-solving. Design is the design for life in time and in context. Design leadership starts with empathy, research, and imagination to define a vision of betterment with quality and extends through all the steps required for its realization. It requires special planning, economic analysis, and communication skills often missing or lacking in design education. It involves bringing many voices together to add their expertise and insight at the right time in the process. Every tool used to document and analyze a project, whether maps, plans, sections, models, animations, spreadsheets, or graphs, all have a bias. Each asks certain questions but may exclude others. It is important that a design leader understands the limitations and power of each representation or model and uses multiple tools to develop a design proposal that responds to the ecological complexity of the context and the diversity of its users.

As a project moves into construction, design leaders help spread and maintain the importance of the work and the ethic of quality to the contractors and sub-contractors. A design leader is the shepherd of the project from its modest beginnings to its full realization.

We know architecture has limits and is but one part of a culture's make-up, but we believe if all architects consider and care for its betterment together, we could have an overwhelming collective impact on the health of our society and environment.

12

RESOLUTE

Do not compromise our design effort to accommodate expediency or mediocrity. Be open to criticism and improvement no matter where we are in the process. Never send out drawings or other instruments of service that are not at the level of our intentions or that are incomplete.

No matter how hard and long we work on a project, our time and effort are minuscule in proportion to the life of a building and its effect on the lives of others. We try to remember that, whether we are in schematic design or checking a shop drawing. Until it is built, we can make it better. We still must make progress. We are still responsible for the budget, schedule, and program. When tested, without enough time, strategy always provides a way forward. In the final days of a schematic design proposal, we may find significant flaws in the design. At this point, we can choose several strategies to protect the quality of the project while we proceed. If we believe that the owner can help us reconcile the flaw, we can present the design with its issues highlighted and involve them in the solution. If we believe the design must fundamentally shift, we may elect to adjust the current deadline to allow time to resolve the design. If there is a critical path schedule, we can shift another interim deadline to maintain the overall schedule. It is hard to rush early design work and easier to catch up during a later design phase when the design ideas and strategies are clearly outlined and underway. In the final days of design development, we may realize we have an issue with the overall shape or assembly. Again, we have strategy choices. We may scale back on the detailing in the deliverables to give us the time to focus on and resolve the problems or again adjust the schedule. The details can always be developed when the design scope is resolved and clear.

If we are strategic with our time and effort, there is always a way to continue to meet the expectations of the project while never sending out work that we do not absolutely believe is worth everyone's consideration.

Presence

SCULLY ASKS US -
TO MEASURE AND RE-MEASURE
CONSIDER AND RE-CONSIDER
PRESENCE IS ENGAGEMENT

Avoid language structures that privilege fast visual communication, novelty, and type. Create rich and elusive forms and spaces to awaken witness to the character and qualities in form.

Experience is thinned by the speed of concept communication, by language, novelty, and typology. Architectural space disappears as we acquiesce to entertainment and make choices in a nominalized world full of instruction and superficial pleasures. We believe architects are world builders. Architects make the places that frame and facilitate our work and play, the places where we reside, meet, eat, learn, debate, consider, and love—where we experience living. Architectural space can stretch us beyond the conditioned slumber of the consumer/media market to expand our senses, our capacity, and our understanding of who we are and who we want to be. Architectural space can promote environmental inquiry and growth.

Strategies to awaken witness in form can be subversive. We utilize indirection and surprise to build resistance, to delay and redirect experience from the quick consumption of language and concepts. We strive to create rich and elusive forms and spaces full of color, light, shadow, weight, lightness, rhythm, and character that engage us with the phenomena of the environment. We strive for form that eludes description and is alive in the environment. We experience buildings in motion, in time, with anticipation, and in memory. If a building is different (darker, heavier, duller, or brighter) than it was yesterday, it opens the possibility of inquiry. It raises questions in our memory, promoting awareness, description, remeasurement in experience, and awakening us to its presence.

BARBER SHOP
254

13

WAKE OF INTEREST

Create a wake of interest. Build desire for our firm and work. Do not market or sell the firm. Let the work serve as an example of our values and passion.

Our early approach to securing new opportunities and clients was to let the work speak for itself. We believed architectural practice was a meritocracy. We believed if we completed projects of quality that served clients and the public, they would be recognized, and we would get more work. Early in the practice, we did receive some follow-up commissions, but eventually, we learned we were somewhat naive. Getting new architectural projects can be, and sometimes is, based on past work, but often, it is not. As time went by, we found competing firms were often hired over us based on their skillful salesmanship and relationships. We also learned that institutions are not always loyal. Even if we do three good projects in a row, university presidents, school superintendents, and government leaders change with political winds. The work to build and maintain these kinds of relationships seemed exhausting. Our problem, like many architects, was that we were particularly bad at marketing, uncomfortable with selling and introductory cold calls, loathsome of lunch meetings with strangers, and neither of us played golf.

Our naivety was, however, productive. For the first several years, we honed our craft, our collaborative process, and our dedication to the communities where we worked. We realized we had to develop a strategy to seek new clients and projects whose objectives and values were aligned with our own. We did not want to sell; we wanted to find a voice for the work that shared its value. Early, we were primarily working for one agency in the state of Mississippi. We were committed to public work. However, for the health of the firm, we also needed to find other public clients whose funds for projects were not tied to the very political state bond bill each year.

While the success of each project is certainly one measure of a firm's worth, in many important ways, it is the firm's values, approach, passion, and integrity that create a wake of interest. We realized we did not have to sell or market finished projects. Instead, we saw that everything we do is marketing. We kept our focus on the work and the communities where it is located. We became better at sharing the project processes and stories, articulating the connections made, the character created, and the search for public value and meaningfulness. We became better at sharing the story of the firm and work.

We did not submit for awards for the first five or six years, believing it was our client's success that defined ours. We eventually realized award programs were another way for us to tell the story of the work and its contribution to our client's missions. We also saw the opportunities to share the work in lectures, community and civic presentations, exhibits, and now, of course, social media. We now understand it is the story of the approach to the work that creates a wake of interest. Over the years, new clients have found us through these stories, and they have become long-term colleagues and friends. They ask us to work with them on multiple projects, and we become a part of each other's extended family.

PROPERTY VALUES

14

DESIGN DEVELOPMENT

Design is a patient search. Experiment. Allow time for strong ideas to take hold. Design is the design of life in all its complexities. Proposals must be rich with potential. Design development is the imaginative work to mature the scope and detail of the work. Preparation of construction documents is the translation of design information into the language of construction.

There is always pressure to deliver work fast. During schematic design, we work to make clear propositions about form and space, shape, and structure. It is the clarity of the propositions that make a good schematic design, but schematic design is immature. It is a statement of values that we have not yet had to fully apply to reality. When the client desires an early date for bidding or starting construction, and we are building the schedule for the project, it is tempting to see the design development phase as expendable and make the mistake of skipping ahead to construction documents. Because we do like to please our clients, we have tried to meet short schedules. It never really works. More often, we end up compensating with long hours in a short schedule. We have learned now to avoid the temptation. The design must be developed, not simply completed. The craft of design work is at its best when it allows the time to be iterative. The first version of the details should rarely be the last.

Design development starts as an exercise in the suspension of disbelief. We pin some things down while we allow others to remain loose, changeable, or unknown. Design development starts by verifying and testing each part of the design. We do design development as an iteration, as a first development of the ideas that is both disciplined and experimental.

Projects move from hopes and desires into form and then into buildable detail. We tell clients often that we can change almost anything during the schematic phase of work. We are still searching for the project. During design development, we are deeply involved in the imaginative making of the project, but some things can be adjusted as we refine the work. When we start the preparation of construction documents, we see this as a translation from design information into the language of construction and, if possible, we do not want to make any changes.

15

SCOPE AND DETAIL

Establish the scope of the work first, then move to details. Add detail to add quality and durability.

Form is both shape and structure. "Scope first, then detail" is a way of ordering the craft of design, a way of thinking, and a practice for quality and economy. For Duvall Decker, this is a model to see shape as a broader category of form more than profile. We see shape as the scope of the character and potential of the project. Scope can be seen as idea, shape, consequence, and strategy. Structure is the make-up of shape, all the materials, systems, and details that are coordinated to make form. Landscape painters say if you get the colors right, you can feel the shape of the space, the character of light, and the sense of place. Space is made and you need less detail to convey quality. Likewise, if the scope of architectural shape is clearly defined, the idea and character of the work are established. The structure and detailing craftwork can be economical and focused on enrichments, where important, and for the quality and resolution of the form.

For the first fifteen years of the firm, most of the projects were procured with traditional design-bid-build delivery. With limited fees and funds for projects, we had to learn to be efficient in how we strategized design ideas and quality. We focused on the scope/shape of the project. We were in search of public value while being very economical in how we detailed a project for construction. This order of the craft of design work also applies to the labor of making construction documents. Documenting the scope before the details ensures more complete systematic construction drawings and specifications. With a clear scope of work, the estimators can accurately bid the project. Then we can work with them on specific details that might need clarification without a change order. When the scope and resources are aligned, the relationship between the contractor and architect can be collaborative.

16

ACCURACY

Accuracy is faster than speed. Slow down, prioritize, be careful, thoughtful, and sure. Mistakes happen when we rush. Mistakes cost much more time and money than any potential savings achieved by rushing.

This is perhaps the most important foundation we have discovered in our studio. In architectural practice, there is so much pressure to move fast, to design fast, to work to deadlines imposed by outside criteria, or to be driven by internal budgets and time allocations. Yet when we rush, we make mistakes that may not be revealed for months or even years. When they are revealed, the time to heal them exponentially exceeds the time that would have prevented them by careful accurate work.

The work to design and realize a building far exceeds the volume and complexity of information and process management for any one person to command. Add to this challenge the pressure to move fast and the likelihood of the loss of design quality and gaps in the craft of the work become extremely high. As buildings become more complex, as architects work for more environmentally mature and sustainable projects, as building systems become integrated, and as we expand the measures of performance, more time is required in the planning and design phases of work to maintain quality and prepare for construction. To us, accuracy is faster than speed means slowing the design process, planning thoroughly, acting with more efficiency, producing comprehensive construction documents, and eliminating issues, conflicts, errors, and unnecessary change orders.

We work to reduce the pressure to rush and to gain design time in many ways. We carefully plan out project schedules to allow both production and reflection. We try not to commit to final due dates until we are confident in the work. We have devised strategies and tools to be more efficient with our time. One of our favorite books is *The Checklist Manifesto* by Atul Gawande.[4] We have checklists to minimize time spent on aspects of every project that are repeatable. We build and use templates for most documents, schedules, budgets, and components of projects that are repeatable. We develop and add to existing resource documents on materials, details, and systems that capitalize on and continue to build our experience.

Architectural design is an iterative process. We utilize an agile management structure to ensure the team evolves the design together in a process that builds on its experiments, research, and achievements. At each phase of work, we document the progress in comprehensive work products. All information is carried forward. At each phase, the work products are evaluated by every team member, validated, and revised, and the design is matured as required. The project evolves from scope and quality information to detail and then construction communication.

JUSTICE
COURT

17

MANAGEMENT

Control the money, time, and scope/quality. Do not start a project if the funds are inadequate, the time is impossible, or the scope is ill-defined. Keep the variables in balance. Budget the project appropriately and check it at each phase.

We have heard many architects say there are three variables to any project: time, money, and the quality of the work. If any one of the variables is out of balance with the others, the project will be challenging. This foundation was written as we were learning how to build a firm and business. We certainly saw the reality of this declaration and were able to follow its guidance, but not always. Many of our clients are non-profits or community agencies that have needs and time but limited funds for design and construction. We see it as a responsibility to the community to support groups like Operation Shoestring, Piney Woods School, the Mississippi Alliance for Non-Profits, or the Mississippi Center for Justice with planning, fundraising for improvements, and design work to build when ready. These clients often need an additional investment of our time to advance their mission. On the contrary, most of the work we do for the National Guard (who want long-life, high-performance, durable buildings and have very clear objectives) offers good, simple design opportunities and results in good cash flow. We learned not to hold each project to the limit of a simplistic project management budget, but to be flexible and see benefits beyond profitability, including community service or opportunities to learn and hone our craft.

In the first few years of practice, we learned how the traditional business model of an architecture design firm can be thin, volatile, and very fragile. We learned to balance the projects, their community/firm value, and cash flow support, but we also realized with our knowledge and skills, we could reimagine the practice and business model to expand the ways in which we work by adding facility management, community planning, development, and development consulting. Each of these activities/services offers unique enhancements and educational benefits for the studio. With this expanded approach to practice, we work with clients before the projects are defined through planning, negotiating for real estate, helping to secure equity and subsidies, and the work carries on through design, construction, and long after by caring for buildings. Each of these engagements offers different fee opportunities with overlapping financial performance benefits, helping make a more robust and sustainable business.

We have learned to see the business as an expanded field of activities. The architectural projects are seen as a body of work, the facility management and development consulting as complementary activities, together all contributing to a more sustainable business. Over twenty-five years, we have never missed a payroll and never failed to share profits through bonuses at the end of the year. (Truth be told, there was one year when we borrowed money to pay bonuses.) As my (Roy) hard-working laborer father used to say, "Take care of others, always do good work, and the money will be there."

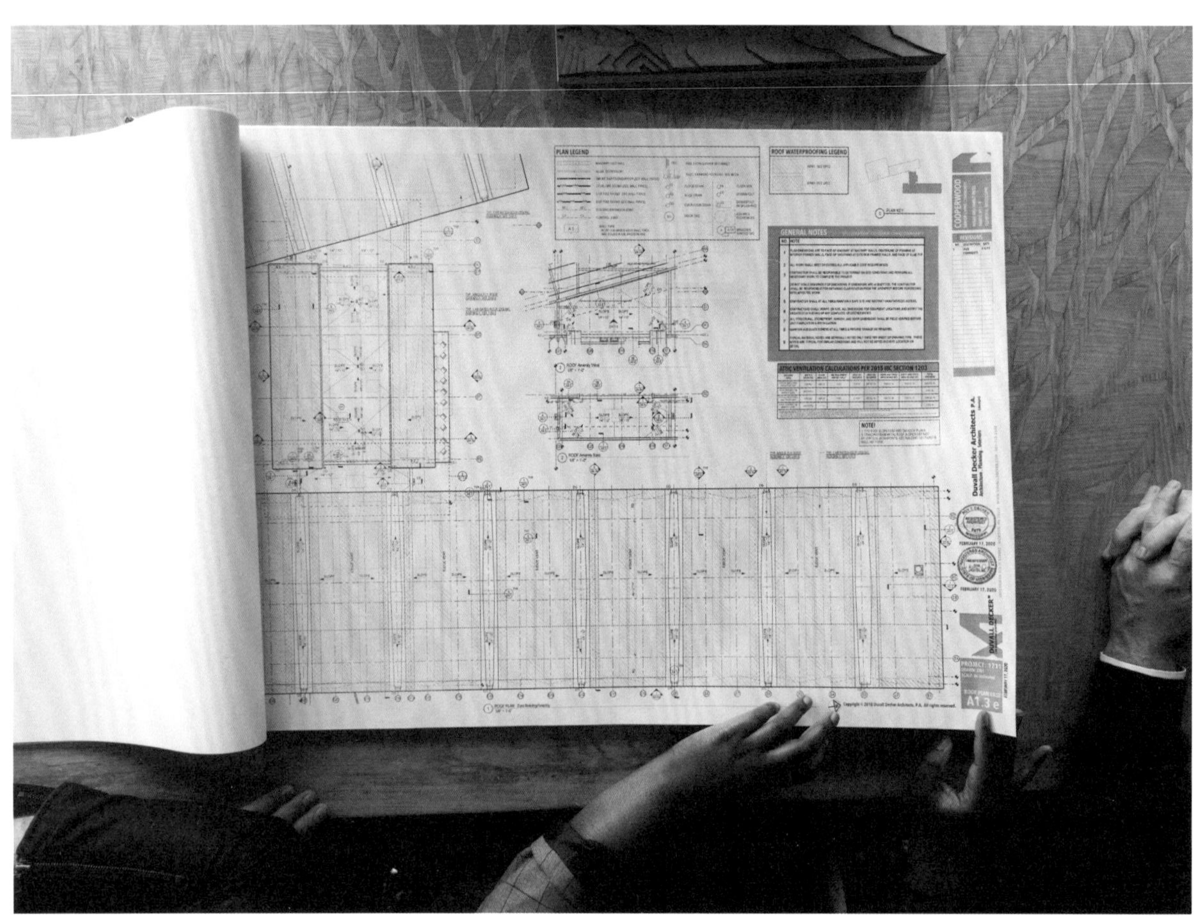

18

TRUST THE WORK

Use the drawings and specifications during construction. Check every decision, every question, every time. "Let's go look at the drawings, specifications, and submittals." Do not feel pressured to answer immediately.

We are continually surprised that even after toiling over a set of construction documents, working through all the detailing, coordinating with engineering systems, and making material finish choices, our team members sometimes forget to trust the work. In the field, standing in front of an apparent conflict, misalignment, or other construction coordination question, with the contractor asking for quick answers to avoid a delay, the pressure is palpable. This is exactly the moment of opportunity to trust the work. This is the moment to not answer but to take the time to check the drawings and specifications. We have never seen an emergency on a project that does not allow time to check the documents and provide the best answer.

The most important lesson for young architects in the field to learn is for them to remember to say to the contractor, "Let's go look at the drawings, specifications, and submittals." Often, someone on the team, maybe a year before, thought about the condition in question and provided guidance. If there is a gap, the act of checking allows all involved to understand the issues and contingent conditions that would need to be considered for the best answer.

Maintaining the discipline for all team members to consult and follow the documents is an important ethic for the architect to enforce throughout the project. Entropy will intervene. The contractor will study the documents and think they know every detail but are managing subcontractors who may not have looked closely at the documents since bidding the project. Young carpenters, masons, and laborers may have never looked at the documents because they are following verbal instructions from superintendents or working with knowledge based on their last experience.

When we were younger and first in the field, it was intimidating for an experienced contractor to tell us we did not know how things really worked and that they had been doing the work in question in a particular way for 20 years. We quickly learned in those moments that the documents were our friends. It is important to remember good construction documents are a description of a particular project's materials, systems, assemblies, and quality. But they also carry proven industry standards, code requirements, a firm's best practices, and lessons learned. All this experience gets embedded into typical details and specifications over time. It is true that there is often a lot to learn from experienced contractors. It is also true that many contractors have developed questionable habits or practices. It is the architect's responsibility to determine the difference and advocate for the quality of the work as described in the documents.

Posture

We aim to ground design work in the spatial/psychological postures through which we navigate life and design spaces to foster opportunities for both envelopment and exposure.

Activities and functions (the things we do) are not the most important criteria for making space. At a more fundamental level, we strive to make space that is grounded in the spatial/psychological postures through which we navigate life. We seek risk and security, independence, and belonging. The psychological postures of spatial experience are established early in infancy. From Adrian Stokes and Melanie Klein, we find a compelling proposition. Our first experiences are encompassing and unselfconscious. We belong. As we grow, we discover independence and imagination, but at the price of exposure and risk. As individuals, we mourn the loss of belonging, but we would not sacrifice imaginative freedom. Stokes and Klein propose that we look at all of life as a process of seeking balance between these first fundamental postures.

In forms that prioritize transactional openness, we design each space to foster both postures in time and by choice. We attempt to make each space multivalent and appeal to these limbic instincts of behavior. An invitation in form allows posture(s) to be inhabited. Each space or network of spaces offers conditions that are enclosing and exposing.

LIBRARY COMMISSION

19

BE FORMAL

Follow the contract. Be formal in all aspects of practice and communication, even on the smallest project. Maintain clear and efficient lines of authority and communicate effectively. Document every aspect of the process with drawings and in writing, make clear submittals, and field reports, and keep notes of all meetings, discussions, and decisions to support a complex team in search of design excellence.

Even the simplest building project is a complex endeavor. Over months or years, hundreds of people may contribute their insight, time, and labor. Individuals and companies put themselves at financial and even physical risk to complete the work. To honor this commitment to quality, it is essential that the agreements and tools that govern how a complex team (owner, the public, architects, engineers, contractors, subcontractors, suppliers, and manufacturers) behaves together are useful, clear, respectful, and maintained in practice.

Early in our practice, we understood the value of being formal with our design partners and in construction. We were diligent about keeping notes, meeting minutes, and coordination lists. Once we started working with larger and more organized clients, we realized a broader and more formal management tool was needed. The outcome was a document we titled the "Basis of Collaboration" (BOC). The BOC is built on the strengths of the AIA contract documents and then adds best practices for design documents, standards for digital, verbal, and written communication, requirements for working with building information modeling to achieve design excellence, and rigorous construction communication protocols.

There are two parts to the Basis of Collaboration: "Part A – Administrative Requirements" (an innocuous title that belies some of the radical disruptors that inspired it—the unprecedented growth of partnering structures, the sharing of in-process work products, and the plethora of communication avenues) and "Part B – Design Process Requirements". The Basis of Collaboration Administrative Requirements expand opportunities for advanced collaboration to achieve design excellence while maintaining a clear structure for contractual roles. Part A is a comprehensive description of communication and data management protocols. It limits the forms of communication that can be relied upon and clarifies which forms are contractual. This distinguishes reliable decisions from the informal and often contradictory exchanges that take place while problems are being identified and solutions are being explored. Part A establishes the protocols for sharing and collectively utilizing design tools, including the building information models, their ownership, limits of accuracy, and agency for best practice. Part B – Design Process Requirements provides design partners with Duvall Decker's process and project requirements for design excellence. It includes document protocols, collaboration standards, and examples.

NES
Rentals

20

FEED THE BIRD

Anticipate the construction process. Construction is a long, slow negotiation. Provide emphasis and critical information at the right time to impact and maintain the construction quality. Too early, and the information will overwhelm. Too late, and well, it is too late.

Years in academia have taught us that only a very small portion of content is retained after an initial lecture. One effective strategy for designing a semester course is to provide an introductory lecture that explains the purpose and value of the work and as the course unfolds, review individual points in depth. As you work with the students, you can make connections to what they have experienced with what is on the horizon. We have found a similar strategy can be effective during construction.

At the beginning of a construction project, there is an enormous amount of information that must be transferred from the architectural team to the construction team. This transfer is usually accomplished through the construction documents. Construction documents include comprehensive information for a project but often do not communicate the hopes, feelings, and design principles that have formed the work and that lie behind the plans, sections, and specifications.

During construction, an architect is charged with observing the progress and quality of the work, providing interpretation of the construction documents, approving payments, and tracking and reporting on the schedule. This arm's length observation of the work is a tradition defined in the contracts and is important for maintaining lines of responsibility and authority for construction. It also assumes contractors are skilled builders, which is not always the case. More often contractors are managers of subcontractors who are often shorthanded and supported by laborers who do not know how to build. Without venturing into the contractor's responsibility and authority for the means and methods of construction, we have developed two strategies beyond simple construction observation to support contractors, add value and knowledge to the project, and help ensure better project craft and quality. First, like the first academic lecture, we present the design to the contractors. We bring them into the story of the project, its origins, goals, and performance requirements. As the work progresses, we conduct in-depth, detailed pre-construction/demonstration/mockup review meetings for each major trade and assembly condition. In each pre-construction meeting, we link more team members to the goals of the project, the ethic, and care for quality. Second, we look ahead at each step of work and anticipate what is required for the contractor to be successful. We add the specific piece of information at the right time to have the most effective impact. Feed the bird. We report our questions, alert the contractor to governing drawings, details, and specifications, and answer any questions they might have prior to the next phase of work getting underway. We review the goals, build on their experiences, and help them see what is over the horizon.

21

CRAFTSMANSHIP

Teach craft. Often the architect knows more about the quality of craftsmanship in materials and construction than the contractor or subcontractor. The ironic thing is that an architect's knowledge is secondhand (head knowledge without the handwork). But by teaching the value of craft and holding the requirements of quality during construction, we help the contractors, laborers, and the industry regain skills and achieve quality in the work.

Richard Sennett, in his book *The Craftsman*, defines craft as a quality embedded in a work that is the result of an investment of skill beyond productive labor. For Sennett, craftsmanship is the "desire to do a job well for its own sake."[5]

When we raise questions on craftsmanship in architecture, we first look to the studio and then to the construction site. In the studio, architectural craftsmanship includes both the process of designing and the production of representations that are utilized to explore proposals. Skills essential for designing start with empathy, research, and listening, followed by exploration, proposals, criticism, iteration, and verification, all leading to refinement. We resist preconceptions and we work with a small set of propositions and a limited palette of materials. We are careful with and critical of the communication tools; the drawings, renderings, models, letters, budgets, contracts, specifications, and ideas, and consider what each form of representation reveals and what it conceals.

To build well, particularly in our region where there is little opportunity for construction skill development and where expectations for building quality are low, is challenging. Public construction today is dominated by a capitalistic formula of fixed scopes of work with contract cost and time limits. This production imperative only requires workers to possess minimal skills to complete tasks. There is little incentive for workers to connect their labor to the increased quality of the work beyond themselves. The result is a determined production process that systemically exploits labor and perpetuates mediocrity.

Architects often do not have hands-on construction skill but do possess a knowledge of construction quality. While we cannot directly demonstrate construction skills, we can provide the goals and quality requirements for masons, metal workers, concrete contractors, and carpenters to practice to be craftspeople. We do this by creating educational opportunities within the construction documents. We specify requirements for pre-construction meetings and detailed craft-focused mockups that we support as teachers. We have found that workers who come to a project ill-trained show a sincere desire and ability to rise to the challenges of improving the quality of their work. We find the loss of craftsmanship in the construction industry has more to do with the capitalistic-driven production imperative and less to do with the limitations of workers wanting to do good work. While we must work through the contract documents, we choose to support the workers in an aspiration for craftsmanship.

22

CHEMISTRY

Chemistry is important. A great project is only achievable if the architect, client, and contractor work together with mutual respect and patience. Do not take the project if the chemistry is not right. It is not worth it, and it will not be a successful project.

We see an architect's larger project as facilitating a process to achieve success for all parties involved. This triad—of the owner, architect, and contractor, a union of three—must manage requirements and resources, establish and achieve goals, and navigate challenges over a long period of time to the benefit of the project. Chemistry can be a prerequisite, but it also can be cultivated and maintained by the architect. We have walked away from good potential projects due to a questionable team member. We have also failed to see a difficult team member or to identify a conflict of interest only to find ourselves in a dysfunctional relationship.

Over the years, we have had instances of an owner/client showing disrespect to our team or asking us to participate in questionable practices. In these cases, it is sometimes best to walk away. Leaving projects once underway can be extremely difficult and stressful. First, you are party to a contract for service and the breaches must be clear. Second, the stress of the loss of the project and fees can be harmful to the financial health of the firm. Several years ago, we were engaged and under contract for a very large project. We had completed schematic design and secured all city and state environmental permits. Without our counsel, the owner entered a relationship with a local contractor. The owner and contractor began a pattern of requests for documents that were not complete. The contractor told us not to worry about completeness, that "he would secure the permit and he knew how to build." We resigned from the commission, cited many breaches in the agreement, and walked away from an important project for the studio and a large design fee. A year later, we heard the contractor's office was raided by the FBI. We made the right decision.

We have also had contractors who did not act in the best interest of the project. An early publicly bid project was won by one of the largest contractors in the country. We were a young, small firm. Within a few months, we realized they were attempting to overwhelm us with change order requests. This was an openly predatory behavior. The problem for this contractor is that we did have complete documents, details, and tight specifications. We also were formal with all communications, had detailed records, and were able to reject all but a verifiable few change requests. In the height of the conflict, the contractor's managing partner told us he would "bury us with the project." Difficult as it was, we did not stray from our commitment to the union of three and the ethic of quality for a successful project. In the end, the project was completed under budget and the contractor corrected all substandard work. Years later, that same managing partner described our firm as one of the best he had ever worked with.

23

MACHINE

Do not borrow money. Work to achieve high-quality buildings within the funds available. Plan carefully and be efficient. Raise fees. Keep the overhead low. Pay staff at the highest rate possible. Maintain a studio that can choose the next project. Do not create a machine that needs to be fed.

Most of the expense for a studio is dedicated to team salaries. This is the greatest investment a firm can make to advance the quality of the work. We pay each team member as high a salary as their education and skill demands and as we can afford. We do operate as a meritocracy and support initiative and skill development with opportunities, salary increases, and bonuses. The remaining overhead expenses are small but we strive to keep them low. This business strategy of investing in the team and keeping all other costs minimal has served us well over the years. The cash flow of an architecture firm is an almost impossible management problem. There are many outside variables that are out of our control. Projects can start, stop, or be canceled. Clients can be slow in paying for services. New projects can walk in the door while you are otherwise committed and tempt you to grow to meet the challenge. We joke, we always seem either six months from bankruptcy or pressured and behind with more work than we can do.

During most of the firm's life, we operated debt-free. There were, however, two periods of time when we broke this foundation, for good reason, but the price was high. The first was after the 2008 fiscal crisis. This downturn hit the health of the firm in 2011. Slowly, over the year, we completed long-term projects and had very little new work to start. In the last quarter of 2011, work was scarce, and we had used our reserves. At the end of the year, we borrowed a good bit of money to make payroll and provide bonuses to the team who had worked hard all year. We knew every business-minded person would tell us that without signed contracts for future work, this decision was crazy, but we kept the team together.

As luck and hard work combined over the course of the following year, we received 26 new commissions. We did not miss a beat and moved on to the new year and work. While borrowing money turned out to be the right thing for the work and firm, it did hurt. It took two years to pay back the loan. Every month over those two following years, the debt payment added to our overhead and stole a little design time.

The second time we borrowed money was after the pandemic. Even with the federal aid in the form of a PPP loan, work slowed and cash flow was challenged. Over the course of 2021 and 2022, we slowly borrowed more cash to make payroll and pay bills, and again, paying it back is painful. Today, with hindsight, we might change this foundation to strive to avoid debt and balance short-term needs with the long-term goals of the firm. Today, we have set new goals for greater reserve funds as we work to pay back the loans we took to recover from the pandemic.

24

TIME

Take time off. Travel, take field trips, and experience cities, buildings, landscapes, and ideas outside of our familiar settings. Keep the practice in perspective. Do not overwork. Protect creative time by controlling the schedule. Protect time off by controlling the schedule.

Architecture is creative but is also technical, tedious, and certainly labor-intensive. We have heard many estimates on the ratio of creative to technical/management work. Some say architects only spend two percent of their time on design. We do not agree with this estimate as it limits the definition of design to concept drawings, diagrams, or renderings of appearance and excludes from design the imaginative work of making a thing real. Appearance is the lowest form of achievement for a project. The craft of design work is alive in every bit of the work. The proposals, alternative studies, reflection, research, planning, making of efficient construction documents, and applying productive criticism are the imaginative work to achieve design excellence.

The dedication it takes to achieve meaningful quality does require time. Design work is both iterative and cyclical. The work can be consuming. We do work hard, but we aim to avoid long hours through the careful scheduling of projects and deadlines. The studio has always been made up of team members who both love and are dedicated to the work. In the early years of the firm, we had a few hard pushes with long hours to get a project complete, but as we gained skill in planning, these almost "all-nighters" were limited and few and far between. It is essential that we keep the work in perspective. We encourage time off; everyone has dedicated illness, holiday, and vacation days each year. Additionally, we include allowances for half-days of flex-time-off to accommodate personal needs from dentist visits and children's events to haircuts and anything else. We empower each team member to oversee their own schedule and work. Everyone schedules their vacation and out-of-the-office time and we work project schedules around them. We have a collaborative office and are organized to support each other.

We believe travel is essential. You might even say it is part of our continued education. The more buildings, sites, landscapes, and cities we experience, the more we feed our intuition and build our insights. We can draw upon these to support our clients and communities with thoughtful design work. On trips for projects, we encourage all team members to add a little time for dinner with a friend, a museum visit, or other non-business experience. Team members are encouraged to take vacation time and share experiences. We believe breaks are important to our health and well-being. As owners of the firm, it has often been hard to follow our own advice, but we have learned that it is least stressful to take our longest family trips at the end of each year when the work and schedules allow a little more flexibility.

Politic

FORMS OF AUTHORITY
INSTRUCTION
SINGULAR
PLURAL
INQUIRY
OPEN

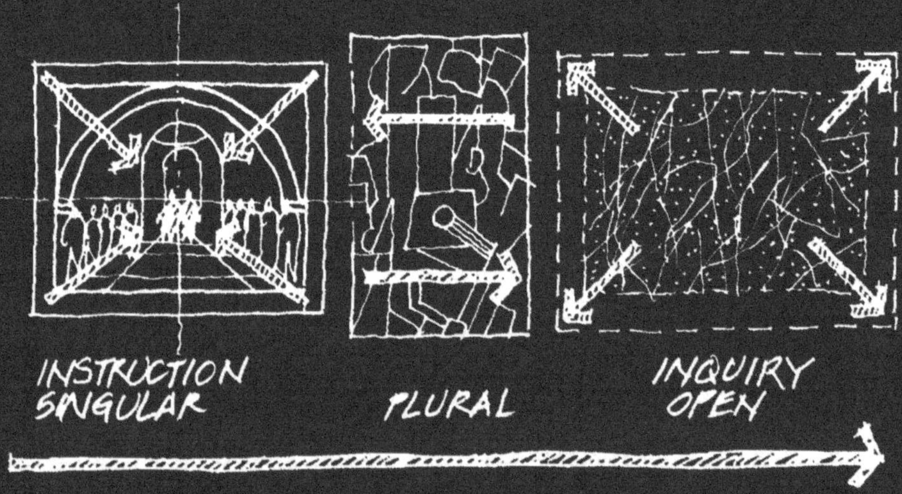

Redistribute the authority in form to empower individual inquiry and growth.

There are many manifestations of authority in form, from hierarchies in cities to the position, scale, and material distinctions between institutions and commercial structures. Traditional structures of authority are based on the power of one group over another. Those not in power are marginalized. Traditionally, figures of power such as religious, civic, and institutional buildings framed private and public space. Today, structures of authority are more hidden and diffused into our lives. We live in a "control society" where political and corporate interests, market instruction, and entertainment assume dominance in characterizing experience and conditioning public behavior. Digital feeds, signs, and commercial forms of identity replace civic experience and legibility. With more instruction, there is less civic engagement, debate, and individual inquiry. Society has become more tribal as truth and fact has become opinion. As experience is characterized by these diffused political, corporate, and market interests, actual public space both disappears and becomes more desirable and therapeutically important.

Architects are responsible not just to act on behalf of the clients, but also for all of those who do not have a seat at the project table—all of those who will encounter, if not inhabit, the buildings and spaces of projects. This responsibility to be both servant and leader requires architects to interrogate the consequences of each proposal for its public value. In this regard, we believe the question of authority in form is one of the most important of our time. We see the injustice inherent in power structures and how that injustice is perpetuated in architectural counterforms. We worry that the very idea of "community" has been compromised by an unhealthy focus on individualism reinforced by selective social feeds and opinions.

Can the divisions and tribalism promoted in national news and social media be undermined and interrogated at local levels to return productive civic debate to the actual issues and problems in our neglected cities? Can architects facilitate and even lead this conversation for a more just, equitable, healthy, and maturely diverse community? We search for opportunities to make space plural and to empower those in the margins. We work to open opportunities for individual inquiry; we search to make public space that can facilitate meeting, diversity, and opportunities for civic experience.

25

COLLABORATE

Maintain a teaching studio. Collaborate. Enrich the project with diverse points of view. Grow a studio of individuals who become excellent generalists.

Roy is a teacher at heart, but in 1998, he left his tenured teaching position. He had become weary of the gap between intensive design education efforts and graduates reporting disillusionment, finding little opportunity for their voice or a priority for design excellence in the firms they joined after graduation.

At the time, I (Anne Marie) proposed we start a firm and see it as an opportunity to teach by example. This simple idea was an important origin of the studio. What would a collaborative, educational studio environment look like when diverse voices are empowered? How would we approach teaching young architects in practice? How could we make a firm that could help train young architects to see architecture as a public project?

Over the years, we have developed some simple practices to immerse young architects in educational experiences to support their growth. First and most important, we encourage their voices to participate in the projects and firm. As we note in Foundation 53, the best idea wins. This means we elevate the importance of the project and its consequences in communities above any one ego and value everyone's insights toward this goal. We listen for the best ideas for projects and for the firm. Like many firms, we maintain informal and formal educational opportunities and encourage outside professional advancement. We are transparent about the operation of the firm, project budgeting, and marketing. When young architects join the studio, they support a more senior team member with completing a project. As they grow, we seek opportunities for them to lead a small project with close support. We also try to engage them in the construction administration process and get them into the field as soon as possible. We have found that field experience is essential for learning to be a design leader. Realizing the heavy consequences of the lines on paper is enlightening. Later, when they lead a project, the senior team member who helped to train them may become their helper. While this sounds sequential and systematic, it rarely is. We are a small firm with many demands and shifting schedules. But while it may not always be clean and sequential, it is the pattern and discipline we follow for the education of young architects. All of us are teachers and all of us students. Along the way, we support the National Council of Architectural Registration Boards' intern development program and ask young architects to keep us informed on any gaps in their experience that we can help to fill. This program to facilitate licensure is a fine record-keeping system but does not make an architect by itself. Our goal is to help young staff members become well-rounded architects.

26

KINSHIP

Develop relationships with owners, consultants, suppliers, and fabricators. Trust them and challenge them. Be loyal to them, and they will be loyal to the studio and work.

When you are completing your first projects, it is tempting to be overly accepting or overly critical of your collaborators—overly accepting when their disciplinary knowledge is exponentially beyond yours, overly critical when they seem rigid or unmovable about requests to adjust or reconsider a system, configuration, or detail. A successful collaboration is determined by respect, openness, and humility. With these skills, we can discern the difference between the stubbornness that comes from deep experience and that which comes from a lack of imagination. In other words, if we are truly respectful, open, and humble, we are more likely to discern if those traits are being exhibited by our collaborators.

It is also important to understand that collaborators are humans, and we are building relationships with them over time. While they, like us, are attempting to practice respect, openness, and humility, they, like us, may fall short in one moment and succeed in the next. Grace is important, as long as it, too, is mutual. If we both are practicing these virtues, over time, our collaborative relationship will be productive and good.

Loyalty, as we look back on writing this foundation, is not really the right term. While the relationship is personal, it is also professional, and the continuation of it depends not just on the shared virtues, but also on a shared ethic about the work. For us, this shared ethic is a belief that the quality and craft of all of our work matters. It matters to us as we work together, and it matters to all others who will be affected by it over time.

Gordin McCool was one of the first mechanical engineers we worked with on our early K-12 schools and the Mississippi Library Commission. We infinitely appreciate the knowledgeable and affable collaboration we enjoyed with Gordin. He is no longer with us, but to this day, we still say, "allriiiiight" when we embark on a challenge, honoring the encouraging sing-song way that Gordin accepted every one of ours.

Wicker Brothers, Inc. is a custom metal fabricator in Florence, Mississippi. Over the years, we have brought them custom metal design problems, and they have taken them on with curiosity and innovation. Can we embed bronze letters in a stainless-steel emblem and set it in a tile floor? Hover letters over custom slumped glass? Create light lenses around windows from single aluminum plates, or build them out of lighter plates assembled on a frame in the shop? They are excited by every challenge we bring them and teach us about the properties, cost, and fabrication of metal with every solution they propose.

We have many collaborators we work with repeatedly. They know us, and we, them. Design is the design of life and no one perspective can capture all others. It is only with a team of collaborative souls who work together that we can hope to achieve design excellence.

27

AVOID NOVELTY

Build on experience. Limit the palette (ideas, materials, and products). Cultivate surprise that can be revealed over time. Avoid novelty for its own sake. There is only one surprise in novelty and little lasting value.

We have found it valuable to distinguish surprise from novelty. Surprise is a disturbance in what we think we know or what our senses are conditioned to expect. Surprise can be an open window to inquiry, where qualities and feelings ignite reflection. We sometimes describe this kind of disturbance as uncanny form, familiar but unfamiliar. Surprise, when sustained, is alive, incomplete, open, an end-in-process. By contrast, novelty is seen as something new or unusual but a fleeting amusement, more akin to spectacle. For us, a novel gesture or condition often leans toward entertainment, marketing, or an egocentric expression. Novelty for its own sake is generally understood as difference without depth, short-lived and complete, an end-in-itself.

Robert Irwin's work was an early and ongoing teacher, particularly as first chronicled in Lawrence Wheschler's book, *Seeing is Forgetting the Name of the Thing One Sees*.[6] Irwin's work seems to us to be a search for art not simply as an object but as a way of perceiving. He connects presence to perceiving and shows how the speed and propensity to nominalize experience can interrupt exploration. His work and thoughts helped us see that form could be the interaction between us and things, over time, or as we came to describe it, the in-between, a condition of witness.

Witnessing Robert Irwin's re-installation at the Whitney, *Scrim veil-Black rectangle-Natural light,* in 2013, was a particularly formative confirmation of the understanding that surprise could be a path to opening perception and inquiry. When form can slow our propensity to apply names or categories to things and people, it can open an awareness of perceiving oneself perceiving, creating a sort of awakening in the ability to appreciate depth and subtle differences. This is a kind of therapeutic vision. When we learn to see past the name, it can lead to more refined perceptual skills and maybe even change how we approach other areas of our lives such as social and political relationships.

An editor at a national architectural magazine once told us our work was not novel enough for its readers. Though it felt like an indictment, she meant no harm. She was serving her market. We realized through that experience that the profession/press/awards programs were often chasing novelty and spectacle, confusing fashion with cultural relevance. We understand that our pursuit of surprise as a method to recondition experience, to see past, present, and anticipation united in a search for meaning and growth, may be too quiet to gain the attention of the market; however, we have faith that the search for an artistic quality that awakens perception will be engaging and impactful in its place over time.

BENNIE G. THOMPSON
ACADEMIC & CIVIL RIGHTS
RESEARCH CENTER

28

ORIGINS

Communities have origins. While often hard to find or forgotten, sometimes valuable, sometimes not, the origins of communities can rarely be denied. Acknowledge origins. Build on the foundations of geography, people, weather, and politics. Be supportive, critical, and/or educational. Remember to do better.

Tougaloo College was founded by the American Missionary Association (AMA) in 1869. AMA's goal was to establish one college in each state where people were forced into the institution of slavery. Prior to the founding of the school, the land had been a plantation maintained by enslaved people. It was widely reported that the former owner, John Boddie, was brutal and abusive to those individuals who worked the land and built his mansion, a building that still commands the center of campus today.

These two origins persist. The historic mansion stands on high ground, a reminder of the land's exploitive origins, yet all around are the structures of an educational institution where human dignity and hope find a future. The memory of the past is one of the sources of inspiration for students to strive for educational excellence and the opportunities it affords. This campus was also one of the philosophical centers of the American Civil Rights movement. Campus leaders courageously provided sanctuary for civil rights activists as they shared ideas, devised strategies, and fought for freedom, equality, and an end to segregation. Ernst Borinski, a lifelong advocate for human and civil rights, taught and inspired many in his social science seminars. Martin Luther King, Jr., Andrew Young, Robert Kennedy, Fannie Lou Hamer, and many others participated in the seminars and spoke from the College's chapel pulpit.

For the design of the Bennie G. Thompson Academic and Research Center, we unknowingly followed the path articulated by bell hooks in her article "Choosing the Margin as a Space of Radical Openness," where she councils us that the deeper function of remembering is to illuminate the past not for nostalgia but to "transform the present."[7]

The project siting and organization fit into and are respectful of the historic campus green and mansion. This posture offers a connection to the past and a ground from which a series of critical departures can emerge. The architectural organization is indirect. There is no single identifiable center, and edges are made occupiable for students and faculty to claim, meet, and talk. The wings of the building are connected by compressed aluminum thresholds clad with larger-than-life images of civil rights events and figures. These thresholds act as memory theaters that press in, embodying a palpable sense of movement from oppression to freedom. They promote pause and reflection in the daily habitation of the building.

Our dear (and missed) friend, Allen Eskew, once characterized this project as an achievement in "progressive vernacular form." We were grateful for his observation. He felt the thickness of time embodied in form, a balance sought between respect for origins and the critical stance for hope.

29

MOCK IT UP

Plan ahead, use mockups as a tool to engage and structure the team and work, record the search, evolve design presentations, deepen design development investigations, and build complete construction documents.

Mockups, from pre-design through construction documents to in situ construction performance mockups, harness the sustained work required to make an imagined thing real. We pursue meaning in the work and mockups are the iterative process that allows us to visualize an end-in-sight without preconceiving an end-in-itself. Each mockup fosters a search and records that search to inform the next steps and to tell the story of the project and its place.

It is hard to imagine that you can mock up a schematic design presentation before the design is set, but mocking up the presentation creates the space to explore the design. Early in the process, design is a cloud of possibilities and potential explorations. In our economy, we have never had the luxury to indulge all of them. We have had to learn to choose our explorations wisely. Defining the scope and character of the final product both opens and focuses the design effort at the same time. All the design contributors can engage in the design, avoid chasing red herrings, and collaborate efficiently.

Coordination of the different trades is the greatest challenge of construction. General contractors are often managers. Trade partners are knowledgeable but are specialists. Laborers and younger trade workers often have limited knowledge of the importance of sequence or an understanding of how to achieve the craftsmanship required. Mockups are essential to achieve construction quality. They provide a bridge to the contractors and subcontractors for the conversation on craftsmanship and quality that is started in the design, details, and specifications.

We require in situ and, whenever possible, coordinated mockups of all components of the enclosure assemblies. These mockups are collaborative and exploratory in part, allowing the contractor and trade partners to contribute means and methods strategies to achieve the goals. The mockups are educational as well, offering the opportunity for the architect, contractor, and trade partners to share insights and teach younger workers why and how to achieve the required quality. We often conduct pre-construction meetings in concert with mockups and approach them as focused seminars on why and how to be successful in the installation of the work. We see this work as an investment in the knowledge and skills of local subcontractors. Over the years, we have worked with subcontractors and laborers on several projects and have seen improved skill, particularly in architectural concrete work, metal craft, and masonry work.

30

LISTEN BUT LEAD

Listen carefully. The client knows more about the program than you do. The consultant knows more about the systems than you do. The contractor knows more about construction than you do. Listen carefully to the details, the implications, and the relations. Enter the world of each discipline, but lead the process because we know more about the whole of the process and design than the client, consultant, or contractor.

Good leaders are active listeners. A leader guides, enables, and motivates team members and others to contribute to a process of discovery. Leaders try to acknowledge their biases, empathize with others, imagine the diverse life circumstances of the people they encounter, and appreciate unique perspectives. Leaders listen for ideas and insight and follow where they lead. Good listening can ensure that the "best idea wins."

People say that good listeners can repeat what others have said. For architects and planners, it is often not enough to repeat the words we have heard, but to listen for what has not been said as well. Spatial and environmental qualities are hard to communicate in words. The passionate and explicit language of building users and community members may seem overly functional, unattainable, or unrelated to the work at hand, but it is all important. Their feelings open the field of work even though they may not fully understand what is possible. Leaders listen and elevate even the quiet voices. Likewise, in the language of structural, mechanical, electrical, and other special disciplines, requirements may seem to limit options for the work. Leaders listen and value each perspective and discipline to lead the entire team and community in the process for the benefit of the quality of the overall project.

Humility and curiosity and listening with empathy are the best virtues of a listener. In the moment of listening, you can let go of your supposed expertise and ask for more descriptions, more comparisons, more examples, and more understanding. Listening with empathy was never more important than in our work on the Baddour Center Transitional Housing for adults with intellectual disabilities. To prepare, we consulted the experts, texts, and guidance available. We tried to acquire the technical knowledge and instructions for the design work, but still felt inadequate to the task. It was not until we spent considerable time with the residents, watched each person interact with each other and the staff, and listened to residents describe how they live and what creates stress in their environments that we could move forward in the design of their homes. We could then join the technical knowledge with the residents' insights to form the character and quality of the space and set the dimensions and relations. The buildings are simple, quiet, and abstract. Social spaces are sized and proportioned carefully to foster safe engagement. The design allows residents the ability to preview a space and retreat, while large windows allow residents to live in harmony with the larger community and natural environment. Private spaces include careful thresholds and connect each resident to the cycles of the day. The residents report that they love their homes, and staff report remarkably few incidents of conflict or distress.

Leverage

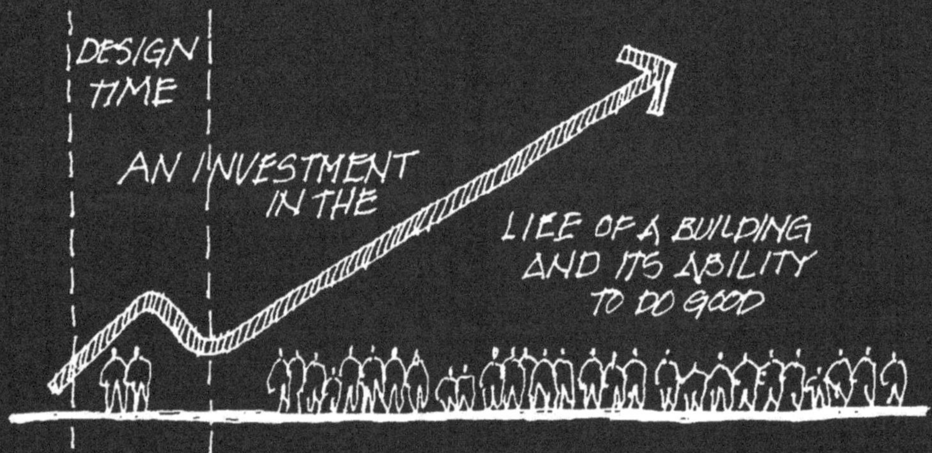
DESIGN TIME
AN INVESTMENT IN THE
LIFE OF A BUILDING AND ITS ABILITY TO DO GOOD

Expand architectural practice, study and engage communities, design for durability, and care for buildings—all to leverage our skills and promote the public good for the full life of a project.

Design time is a relatively small percentage of an architectural project and nanoscale in relation to the life of a building. Duvall Decker is an expanded practice to leverage our skills for greater impact over the full life of buildings. In all these endeavors, we form a bond with our clients and the communities in which we work. We become known for our commitment as long-term stewards and partners.

We are students of communities. Through planning and development work, we support conversations on how to plan for healthy revitalization. We engage communities to ensure that interventions are community-led and action-oriented and instigate open-ended, healthy community growth. To revive disenfranchised, functionally segregated inner cities, we promote density, mature diversity, and mixed-use and mixed-income community developments.

In the state of Mississippi, funds to build are rare and often inadequate, and funds to properly maintain buildings are rarer still. Architectural designs must be long-term investments that grow in value and remain useful over time. For us, the idea of continued usefulness means three things: build with durable materials and design with open infrastructure; make flexible, loose-fit plans; and engage forms and environments. We utilize a simple palette of materials, reused to capitalize on their economy. This leverages our growing construction and detailing experience and increases quality from project to project. We work to make buildings, spaces, and sites that are engaging and alive. We avoid spectacle, borrowed language, or applied narrative. We keep the work quiet, fitting in and not fitting in, born from research and the site of the work. A durable, loose-fitting building that is alive and enigmatic is one that lasts. A structure that is durable in material and memory is sustainable.

We provide facilities maintenance services to care for occupied buildings to allow our clients to focus on their missions well after the design project is complete. Architects know a lot about maintenance, building care, and service, but rarely utilize this knowledge for the benefit of their clients. Caring for buildings provides an important service to clients and an educational opportunity for the design team to learn how to better design long-term buildings.

31

SUCCESS

Measure success by our client's satisfaction and joy, not by awards programs.

We are fortunate to serve a diverse group of clients and to complete multiple projects for some of them over many years. Most of our clients are public agencies or clients who provide public services. They include the General Services Administration, the National Parks Service, the Mississippi Department of Transportation, the Jackson Housing Authority, the Mississippi Military Department, private and public schools (K-12 and higher education institutions), non-profit organizations, municipalities, individuals, and affordable housing developers. In each case, we seek to understand, support, and amplify their public missions for public value.

It is a joy to visit Operation Shoestring to witness the children in the afterschool program. It is a delight to learn that a Methodist pastor chooses to write his sermons in the Mississippi Library Commission or to witness the residents of the Baddour Transitional Homes proudly offer tours to visitors. It is also important to measure benefits beyond the lot lines of the project into the community. In the Midtown neighborhood in Jackson, the community planning work we completed in 2011 provided a strategic road map for the revival of this blighted and troubled neighborhood. The plan identified development interventions that were designed to ignite private investment. The planning work included leadership training for committed residents and helped form many partnerships, including the local college business school. Since the planning work, multiple new affordable housing projects have been completed, new businesses have been started, crime is down, and for the first time in years, Midtown is attracting new homeowners who are able to secure home financing from local banks. These are stories of success.

We have learned the value of submitting projects for awards. Each entry offers an opportunity to document the project and reflect on its strengths and weaknesses. If the project wins an award, we certainly celebrate with our clients and our team. If it does not win, we remind ourselves of this foundation.

32

SERVANT LEADER

An architect does more than provide a service. An architect is a servant leader, which for us, has come to mean a teacher. A teacher reveals the public good when others cannot see it. A teacher explains the value of durability when the prevailing interest is in superficiality. A teacher strives for seriousness in a time of triviality. A teacher promotes diversity, equity, and social and environmental health even in the face of division and exploitation.

We believe the opportunity to design the built environment is a privilege that comes with public responsibility. For us, architecture is both a radical act of service and a hopeful artistic speculation. In every project, no matter its size, type, or budget, architects can expose needs and design strategies to heal, build upon the beauty of place, add value, and elevate human experience. Architectural projects are local and come to be within a specific place and a unique community. As architects, we sometimes do not realize the public consequences that every building or landscape intervention carries. To expand our focus from the project-specific requirements, we ask questions that reframe our perspective. With every project, we ask ourselves, "What is the public value of each decision? How can the constructed environment be critical, healthy, educational, and perhaps, therapeutic for a place and its inhabitants?"

Asking these questions places design leadership in service of public good. We see this special class of leadership as more akin to teaching. Architects, planners, and landscape architects possess special knowledge and skills to lead design conversations to improve our settlements, landscapes, and environment. Each has the ability to see beyond the immediate project needs, status quo expectations, and basic compliance to incorporate improvements to social, economic, political, and environmental space. Design leadership, like teaching, is the imaginative work to guide the team—owner, architect, special consultants, governing agencies, and public—through a cooperative design conversation that leads to more than a functional solution. Design affects all of life and engenders a broad striving for projects to serve their purpose and their communities. The work must be equitable, durable, maintainable, sustainable, energy-efficient, flexible for long-term use, encourage social interaction and education, and connect occupants, visitors, and communities in meaningful ways. Through all of this striving, we hope to create buildings that people want to be in and around, that satisfy purpose with joy.

33

DISCIPLINE

Principles are most important when they are hard to hold.

This foundation appeared when we were faced with difficult situations. We would take a stand to uphold truth, fairness, or goodness. It is a true and aspirational statement and encourages us to do the right thing no matter the consequences. When a large contractor threatened our small business because we would not support a bogus change order request, we fortified ourselves with this statement and would not yield. When our contract was breached by a client whose board consisted of many influential people, we fortified ourselves with this statement and documented the breach in a letter, not because it would benefit us in any way, but just because we believed the record should be accurate and complete.

Early in our work, if the challenge escalated, we would follow this statement with an additional statement of judgment: "You maintain integrity every day, but you only lose it once." But after working with people, institutions, and communities over long periods of time, after being exposed to incredibly complex situations with more nuanced risk and benefit outcomes, after teaching ourselves to respect and understand diverse perspectives, and after witnessing our current society's often quick and simplistic tendency for black and white judgments, we do not offer this statement anymore. We still believe and work to hold principles, and we act on them no matter the consequences, but we do not believe that integrity is so easily judged or so completely maintained or lost. Human beings, even very well-intentioned ones, should not be held to any standard of perfection as judged by any group or individual.

Now, we are more likely to follow this foundation up with the statement, "It is not your mistakes that define you, but how you remedy them."

34

RESEARCH

Learn through experience and research. Identify the specific questions whose answers could help provide direction, meaning, or a technical solution. Allow research to be expansive and educational. Document your work so that it can be shared and expanded.

Conceiving a work of architecture and bringing it into reality may feel like original work, and some of it may be, but most of it is not. We believe architecture is informed by the past, anchored in the present, and speculative about how the future can be better. The long histories of art, architecture, and building, the historical, physical, and cultural conditions of the places in which we build, and the often-opaque relations between causes and effects of phenomena lead us to learn through experience and research, both quantitative and qualitative, disciplined and loose. Intuition is a gift, but it can only be matured through the interrogated experience that is research.

The contract for the new U.S. Courthouse in Greenville, Mississippi required the design to incorporate hundreds of pages of performance standards, functional adjacencies, security requirements, and material and finish guidelines. Little in the project requirements asked us to respond to the social, cultural, economic, and demographic history and conditions of the project's particular place.

To broaden and deepen the expectations for the project, to respect the context both past and present, and to propose a courthouse form for its place, we included an architectural historian, Michael Fazio, Ph.D., on our team. We charged him with researching the social and cultural history of Greenville, the history of the court as an ideological force in the Delta and beyond, and documenting the architectural history as a witness to this story.

Dr. Fazio's essay was powerful. It illuminated the complexity of the community, its people, and its history. It revealed that Greenville has been populated by many different people of varied ethnic backgrounds. It was historically a diverse and cosmopolitan city. Greenville's early prosperity was fueled by an economy made possible by the inhuman practice of slavery, and later, exploitive sharecropping. Now the city's socioeconomic status is disproportionately poor for its majority black population. During the latter part of the 1960s, the court, under the leadership of Judge William Keady, was known to provide all citizens the protections and due process defined by the Constitution. Many cases were decided in this court that changed our country with important decisions regarding voting rights, school desegregation, and prison reform. It was only with the clarity and weight of this research that we could break through the stylistic preconceptions and extend beyond the functional performance priorities initially framed in the project's formal and informal briefs. We could make a design case for a respectful but progressive courthouse that expresses access to justice while it demonstrates the importance of the Court.

35

INSTITUTIONAL MEMORY

Institutional memory is the keeping of records (in digital and/or paper form) of anything we do in our daily tasks that could be done again or referenced again to improve business efficiency and to harvest knowledge from past projects to produce better future work. Everyone's basic responsibility is to utilize and maintain this institutional memory to avoid re-inventing the already invented and to foster innovation. All our work is valuable beyond the task at hand if we record it clearly and make it accessible to others.

As human beings have taken on increasingly complex endeavors in our technologically enhanced world, a single person cannot complete these endeavors without aid. Atul Gawande writes about the advent of the checklist, the deceptively simple tool that transformed the failed Boeing Model 299 airplane into the notoriously reliable B-17 Flying Fortress. This story about the value of institutional memory documented how teams of people can make extraordinary things happen.

In our Office Policy, we describe the best practices for creating "Instruments of Service." These are the products of daily work. To push the limits and protect creative time, the basics must be managed with deliberate ease. While we are developing, designing, constructing, or maintaining built environments, many of our products are our means—our clear, formal, and recorded communications (letters, e-mails, programs, estimates, drawings, specifications, meeting minutes, field reports, etc.). The ethic we establish in creating and recording this information promotes the ethic of the building's design, construction, and maintenance and builds the firm's institutional memory to expand our collective knowledge.

In addition to formally communicating and documenting our daily work, we generate standards, checklists, templates, and research documents. If we can reduce the amount of time thinking about something we have done before to focus on something we have not, we have a better chance to accomplish something innovative. We have created and continue to develop checklists for each phase of work, site visits, engineering coordination, specifications writing, contracts, managing collaboration for design excellence, and even cleaning our not-so-user-friendly coffee pot.

Our strategy of creating institutional memory leverages the lessons of our experience to buy design time and innovation for every project in the firm.

36

ENTANGLEMENT

We need only consider our own breath to understand how we ground existence within the infinity of time and space. We take in a breath from the infinite, and it gives sustenance to the finite—neither can be made more or less by the interaction, but it is the interaction that brings life. We are all involved in the maintenance of the process. We either promote or suppress it. Our breath is space and time, and in breathing it, we dwell in it. If our lungs cease to support the interaction, we die. In art and architecture, the things that we create should promote the interaction. The concrete must breathe the abstract. The known must breathe the unknown. The present must breathe the future and the past.

We often say that everything is a world to be studied and understood. We also often say that architects are world-builders. These two statements, which seem like they would mutually exclude one another, exist together in cognitive dissonance, much like the idea of being a servant leader.

The living and breathing circumstances of a project exert themselves upon the design solution over time. The history of the site, the qualities of the landscape, city, or neighborhood and its people, the character of the environment, the program for the project, the budget and economy, the skills of the workforce, the mission and skills of the client, the perspectives and skills of the design team, the properties of materials, gravity, sun, water, and soil, and the expectations of society all have the ability to both inform and be transformed through the work.

Design is an attempt to enter the world of the project and make an intervention. This can seem like an independent act, but it is not, just as the designers can seem like independent beings, but they are not. Creative intentions infuse the things we make with character. They also join in and add their voice to an established world. With each intervention, a change is made in the indescribable, full-bodied character and experience of a place.

Consider the experience of a performance of an Eric Satie composition, *Pieces Froides*.[8] The music is composed of notes, harmonies, repeating figures, and rhythms, but it is also performed with adjustment, exception, and variation. While the form and shape of the composition is apparently complete on the paper, the composer's performance instruction to "play painfully" opens the work and invites the specific circumstances of the performer, place, time, and people to affect its character. It is infused with creative intention that is open and indescribable in experience.

Inquiry

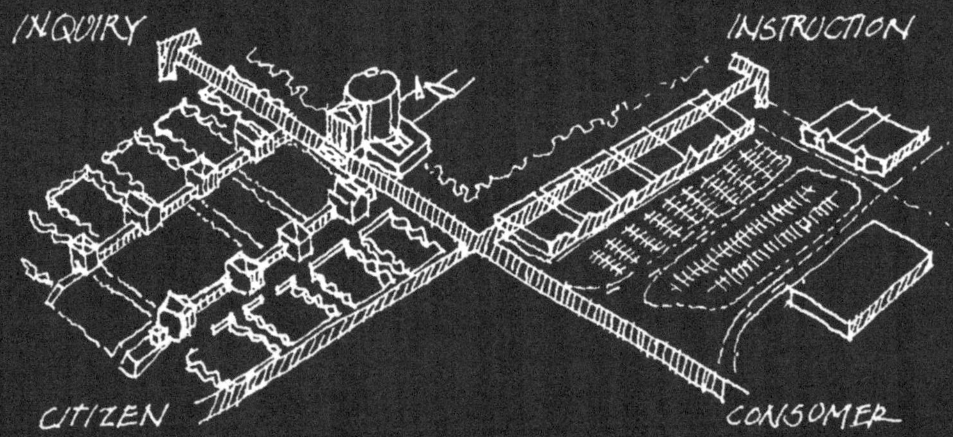

The practice of architecture is servant leadership, which for us, has come to mean a teacher: a teacher leading the design team, a teacher in the work, and a teacher during construction.

Cities, landscapes, and buildings are also teachers. They frame our interaction. They articulate our values. They can facilitate or inhibit social life. We learn what is private, public, shared, and negotiable. Our work as architects is to make physical forms and spaces that promote the best of human possibilities.

We believe in cultural growth. Growth, however, is not possible without criticism, resistance, and proposals that promote active inquiry. We witness how authoritative structures of consumerism can rob us of engaged spatial experience. We work to make forms and space that awaken the slumbering subject. We work to create projects that are scaffolds for inquiry. We strive for mixed-use, diverse, spatial circumstances in character-filled environments. We see this work as therapeutic.

In our region of unskilled labor, we try to support the growth of construction skill and handwork. Today's contractors are managers who hire marginally skilled subcontractors to complete the actual work. We have no unions, few trade schools, and even fewer apprenticeship programs. In traditional contracts, means and methods are separated from the architect's responsibility. Because the contractor is at risk for performance, they are solely charged with the means and methods of construction, but they often have only rudimentary knowledge and skills. The quality of building construction often suffers. We have developed a scope of construction work that includes training, performance standards, and practice mock-ups designed to develop skill and an ethic of craft on all projects. While an architect's knowledge is second-hand, together with a contractor, we can develop a level of craftsmanship that is superior to the status quo. Over twenty years, we have seen this approach bear fruit. Contractors in the area have developed exceptional skill in architectural concrete work, masonry, and metalwork and have carried these skills and this ethic on to future jobs.

37

INNOVATION

Start with doubt—listen, research, and analyze. Continue with faith. Identify the problems and opportunities and make proposals to address them. Suspend your disbelief. Free yourself from preconceptions. Resist the urge to find answers in precedents. Precedents can be valuable, but early, they can be blinding. If we aspire to improve to do better, we must pursue form through the discoveries that emerge from the research, from the experiments, and through the search.

For design work to be meaningful, it requires a critical stance. We immerse ourselves in the place, history, and climate, and engage with the aspirations of the community. We experiment with formal questions that speculate on an aspect of the work, often with a focus on social, political, environmental, and/or philosophical investigations. These kinds of speculative proposals are provocative and educational and when utilized as a tool, are then factored back through the time, place, and program of the work.

As part of the design search for the Mississippi Library Commission Headquarters, we experimented with architectural spaces and sequences that could shift authority from the traditional expression of the power of institutions to the authority of each individual and invite the exploration of spaces with freedom. This study resulted in what we called an indirect plan with pause and move sequences. The spatial organization was one we hoped would promote inquiry and discovery in lieu of instruction and explanation.

Before the design phase for the new U.S. Courthouse in Greenville, Mississippi had even begun, there were charges and expectations for the building to be a neoclassical artifice, a statement of federal power and identity. A recently completed courthouse in Alabama was suggested as a direct precedent to follow. With our knowledge of Greenville, we knew we had to engage our doubt and prove through research and analysis that the preconceived expectations to recreate this neoclassical precedent would have been a bombastic insult to this community.

Prior to the Civil War, Greenville, Mississippi was a prosperous lumber and cotton port. Its prosperity was underpinned by the forced labor of enslaved peoples. After the Civil War, Greenville's prosperity continued, supported by the labor of an exploitive share-cropping system. This is a place where justice has not been equally accessible to all. By researching the story of the place and its people, we broadened the criteria for the project and shifted the project team's expectations from architectural form that expressed "power and identity" to one that expressed "importance and access." We went forward with faith that the team could discover form that would be meaningful in the Greenville community, would promote the justice promised by the Federal Courts, and would fulfill GSA's charge for design excellence that was built on Daniel Patrick Moynihan's guiding principles to express democracy as a living process.[9]

38

RELEVANCY

The movement towards and emphasis on service is also a movement away from leadership and, in turn, relevancy. Architects now ask how to regain public value. Value cannot be claimed, it must be created. This means risk and leadership. This is a path to relevancy.

Early in our practice, we worked often for the State of Mississippi on university campuses and state agency buildings. The state agency responsible for all capital improvement projects at the time was the "Bureau of Building, Grounds and Real Property Management". They would work with the universities and agencies to program, plan, choose project sites, and set budgets. They would then prepare the request for funding from the state legislature. Only after the projects were funded would a request for qualifications for architectural services be issued. Both the Mississippi Library Commission and the Mississippi Department of Information Technology Services projects were products of this process and were sited on a pastoral state campus northeast of downtown Jackson. We felt at the time that the siting outside of the city proper reduced the potential for the buildings to have more public impact, but the decision had been made. The opportunity to help build a more vibrant urban environment in the center of the State's capital city was lost before the architects were engaged.

As our practice matured, we worked to be more involved in the planning, programming, site selection, and even financing of projects before they were defined. We worked with communities on planning, with institutions on programming and budgeting, and with private owners on securing equity and development incentives. We have also completed several small developments where we were at financial risk. As we honed these skills, we observed more clients and communities coming to us to assist them in pre-planning for projects. We had demonstrated value. We now often work as both a development consultant and planner/architect on projects.

39

FORM

Form, for us, is neither the thing nor its consumption. We work for the space, the nature, and the quality of the transactions between.

Form is traditionally defined as the "shape and structure" of a thing. Shape is described as the figure or profile, and structure is its make-up, the arrangement of materials and systems. Architects often arrange use, site conditions, materials, enclosure systems, structure, and other aspects of a building into a particular shape. They employ organizational and compositional orders, grids, and modules to provide guidance. They can too often measure success internally to a project, with a bias toward structure, its functionality, budget, efficiency, aesthetic quality, formal or structural logic, quantifiable public benefits, and performance goals. In this complicated work of making, the potential benefit and voice of shape, as a meaningful aspect of form, can be neglected.

When we consider the public life of a building/site and its habitation/use beyond its making, we see the possibility of another site for "form" outside of the craft of architectural making. This might lead us to a meaningful connection to the natural, historical, social, psychological, and political space of a particular place.

Many years ago, while teaching, I (Roy) had the good fortune to participate in a conversation with artist Robert Irwin, architect Chris Risher, Jr., and a group of fifth-year architecture students at the Jackson Center of Mississippi State University's School of Architecture. The night before, Mr. Irwin delivered an inspiring lecture on his work to resist the numbing effects of nominalization and create a field of experience that could therapeutically awaken and expand a subject's perceptual apparatus. The morning conversation was an expanded exploration of the site of form. Both Irwin and Risher were critical of internal, object-centric formalisms as a conceit of designers. They proposed that our concept-filled world of instructions dulls perceptual capacity. The conversation considered the public, therapeutic value of awakening the subject. For Irwin, as with abstract expressionist painters, this involved making an elusive field that opens perception and leads to heightened curiosity and inquiry. For Risher, a southerner, an architect, and an elusive figure himself, it was additionally important to cultivate shape as an uncanny (familiar and unfamiliar) appeal and challenge to a nominalized world of figures. Both Irwin and Risher understood that for such a creative pursuit to be valuable, the site of form must be in between habitation and building. This strategy leads to the search for form that is in the environmentally alive space of possibilities and contingencies. Here, a bloom of qualities and conditions can continue to raise questions in experience, challenge perception, and lead to inquiry and critical insights over time. This is the space of witness.

40

PUBLIC VALUE

The establishment of the service professional has developed as a criticism of the modern utopian project for architecture. This trend has robbed architects of the purpose (value) of architecture. A service architect, working without a culturally critical (educational) position, will be seen as necessary but not valuable. Many architects suffer a loss of "why."

One night a few months ago, we had dinner with our good friend Paul Mankins, FAIA. Paul is an accomplished architect, a teacher, and a professional leader and is one of the founding partners of Substance Architecture in Des Moines, Iowa. A state and national AIA leader, a winner of the AIA's Award for Excellence in Public Architecture, and a recent chair of the Committee on Design, Paul is a lifelong student of architecture and practice. The dinner conversation touched on many subjects, mutual friends, their newest works, good buildings we had the privilege of visiting, and the general state of society and practice.

In talking about the profession, Paul observed in his experience over the years that he has seen three general types of firms. First are the service firms. There are many of them all over the country doing important and needed work every day to make safe, healthy buildings. Second, there are the design firms doing exquisite work that we might deem good examples of things we have seen before. These are excellent, talented, and technically skillful architects, designing and making great projects. Last, there are the firms with a point-of-view. There are not many, but these are the firms that we find most inspiring as they provide responsible service, are excellent designers, and then ask more of their work. They pursue a passion, whether technical, environmental, or cultural. They push the work to be critical and educationally productive, and, in these efforts, they offer invaluable gifts to their communities and to fellow designers.

For us, this foundation has always been a reminder to push the work beyond program and shelter to seek form that creates public value and is culturally meaningful. We consider and discuss Paul's assessment of firms often. We try to consider the points-of-view in the work we admire and hope we are practicing with a point-of-view ourselves.

MIDTOWN —

41

COMMUNITY

Communities have origins, stories, connections to family, institutions, land, and weather. They function or fail in a particular economy. Effective planning begins with a commitment to listening and research. Communities are complex organisms made up of human transactions, both private and public. Understanding the deeper needs, stresses, and desires that characterize a community is essential to fostering its healthy revival and growth.

Communities are dynamic living organisms. Over time, we have developed an approach to community planning that avoids the trappings of reductive analysis and instead promotes organic, open-ended growth. We start with community engagement for insight into the life, assets, and stresses of a community. Residents, business owners, and leaders have the most valuable information on the history and current health of their community. Informed by the engagement, we then follow with an analysis of the entire system. To understand complex systems, it is useful to take them apart. We isolate components to test their condition, to search for interrelated conflicts, dependencies, and priorities, and we find ways to represent each component on a map. Each community is different, and the choice of components will vary. During the analysis, we find it important to resist making singular proposals on any components. We layer component maps to facilitate a multivariate analysis of the entire system. We identify assets and liabilities across the system and search for opportunities to make strategic interventions that leverage assets and reduce or eliminate liabilities to positively affect the social, economic, and environmental health of the entire community.

Years ago, during a community meeting for one of our first planning projects in West Jackson, we were talking with residents about the needs of the community. There were many ideas for improvements including parks, infrastructure, better communication with police, a community center, etc. During the conversation, an elderly woman quietly told the group that none of their ideas were possible if we did not fix the real problem. Due to the blight and crime in the neighborhood, property values had plummeted, and the appraisal value of her home was now below the balance of her mortgage debt. She, like many of her neighbors, was trapped by debt.

What we discovered was a determinant component of the entire system, one that limited the health of the community at large. We felt naive. We were sure economists and many others understood that in a capitalistic market-based society, private land ownership is a foundation of a community's micro-economy. We adjusted our planning focus and prioritized finding creative ways to stabilize and grow land value. We began searching for strategic re-investments that could increase appraisal values. In at-risk communities, the land can be the most powerful potential agent for change and one of the most valuable resources. The challenge then is how to increase property values to positively affect other components of the system while protecting current landowners from the effects of gentrification.

42

FIRST TEN PERCENT

The foundations of innovation are established quickly. Ideas flow early from desire, need, and opportunity. Most project requirements are defined in the first ten percent of the time of work. Sites, budgets, scope, and even aspirations are often defined before an architect is hired and after the potential for innovation has passed. It is not graphic talent that makes a great project possible. It is the planning before the project is designed.

Many architectural projects arrive in our office already defined and often flawed. They are the result of legislative, bureaucratic, financial, or programmatic processes that we are unlikely to change. We, like many architects, will spend the time, whether paid or not, to interrogate the first ten percent assumptions provided. We look at the opportunities and challenges and propose better project definitions.

Our first public school projects in rural Mississippi were products of the Mississippi State Legislature's "adequate education program." The Department of Education prepared detailed programs and requirements for each project. The requirements for our school projects set the number and size of the classrooms, required a six-foot-wide corridor with visible control by the principal's office, and limited each classroom to one three-foot by six-foot window. The staff members who were creating these criteria were not charged with promoting the design of inspiring educational environments. They were charged with mitigating risk. They doubted architects' abilities to design engaging educational spaces and remain under budget.

In rethinking the Department of Education requirements, we had to make proposals that described the positive effects of natural light on well-being and learning. We had to argue against the potentially detrimental authoritarian and disciplinary message of the principal's imposing profile at the end of a long dark corridor. To make minor adjustments, we had to submit formal change applications with detailed drawings, justifications, and affidavits stating that all other requirements would still be met. In the end, we were able to provide three windows in each classroom and offset the corridor from the imposing figure of the principal. The absurdity of this situation is not the revision process but the fact that architects and educators were not included in the programming and budgeting process or that architects were not simply charged with the goal of designing the best educational facility within the budget.

One of the motivations for expanding our practice was to be involved in the first ten percent of time for every project. We now support institutions and organizations with planning, community engagement, programming, and financial analysis of projects before they are defined. As part of an initial planning team, we can help ensure the project parameters—scope of work, budget, schedule, and site—will all foster a vibrant successful project that serves its community.

Resonance

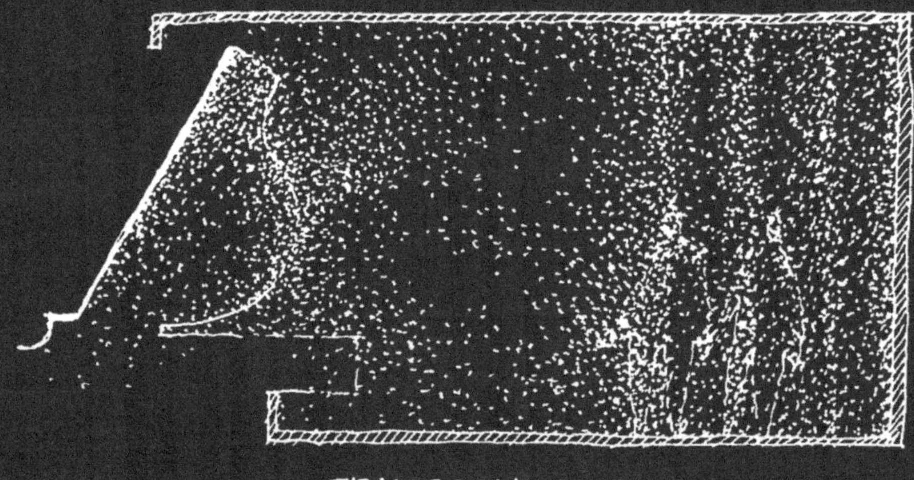

“Sound echoes through the chamber and I feel it in my bones...” is the introductory sentence of a poem written about the experience of the Bennie G. Thompson Center at Tougaloo College.

Humans can amplify measurable phenomena by identifying the natural frequency of a system and introducing an action of matching frequency. We can do this with sound, electricity, and mechanics. The aligning of frequencies is described as sympathetic. A sympathetic action amplifies a phenomenon.

The conditions that allow a musical note to make a sound are a set of ideal relationships put at play in the physical world. The length, material, diameter, and tension of a violin string can predict the perfect form of a particular musical note. This perfect form of a note is only a set of physical and mathematical concepts until you pull a bow across the string. Vibration allows the note to exist, to sound, to resonate in the chamber of the instrument—an abstract idea made real. It is no longer perfect or ideal, but it is vibrating within physical reality. At the same time, the instrument is no longer concrete. It is somehow more than that.

In a scientific example of resonance, the system is simple and isolated to accurately identify the conditions and confirm the results. In art and architecture, the system is the whole of culture and environment in all of its hard-to-isolate conditions, histories, and phenomena. Sympathetic artistic action(s) are necessarily plural. When we witness resonance, from the scientific to the artistic, it is wondrous! A single system in space and time is broadened and made greater by sympathetic action.

People, the environment, and all of the things we create share common experiences. These are sympathetic. We attempt to identify and incorporate these sympathies to amplify them in experience: art, geology, history, mathematics, biology, sociology, weather, physics, etc. Awareness of the amplification of these sympathies can foster those sublime experiences when we are individually present in the specific time, space, and matter of a moment, and also awed by the sense that we are part of something more.

Some sympathies are incorporated as shape. Some are incorporated as structure. Hopefully, they are incorporated to reveal the fallacy of making distinctions between shape and structure, subject, object, and environment.

43

CULTIVATION

Ideas require cultivation, growth, and maintenance. For us, the flow of design work moves from the freedom of proposing to planning and the iterative craft of making to care and maintenance.

We use the term "cultivation" in appreciation of its agrarian roots. The wondrous gifts of this world are our joys, but the sustenance they provide requires nourishment. Similarly, while we wonder at the raw creative talents that many of us have been given, we expect these gifts to be used responsibly.

We often hear architectural projects justified by signature architects making novel concept statements, translated into a simplistic formal diagram, which are then too often built. We fear those early inspirations for what they are—first feelings and simplistic concepts. We believe those early "concepts" require testing and research to gauge their reality and potential value. Maturing these early concepts into meaningful architectural ideas requires engaging in all the materials and phenomena of the environment, acknowledging bodily senses and emotional aspirations, interrogating histories, and speculating upon our culture.

When we started the practice, we had this dissonant combination of bold aspiration and quiet patience. I (Anne Marie) remember, in the first year of Duvall Decker's existence, working in the attic studio and listening to popular music. I think it was Sting's *Soul Cages* album. I was emotionally moved by the music, and I remember the aching realization that learning to create forms and spaces that might foster that sort of artistic experience was going to take time. I also understood the difference between the responsibility of composing music and composing architecture. Architecture impacts individuals and communities even though they did not make the choice to select, purchase, or press play. Buildings are public. They have functional and technical requirements and must be built durably to last. The complex assembly of materials and labor requires the orchestration of design team members, the client, the public, regulatory reviewers, and then contractors. The complexity seemed daunting. How could we achieve the transient artistic feeling I felt from the music? I understood at the time we had to model a design process that allowed us to cultivate our best proposals to match our aspirations. For us, architectural practice and building projects are expansive. Ideas had to be formed that were rich enough to model life. In this way, ideas are not "concepts." They are seeded from intuition and experience and cultivated with research. Ideas are iterated and evolved in each project like crops rotated in the soil from season to season. If cultivated responsibly, each will contribute to the health and quality of the next.

44

IMAGINATION

Imagination is the work to make a thing real.

Foveal vision, the focus at the center of the cone of vision, represents only about two percent of the visual field. This center of the retina is dominated by cone cells which enable high visual acuity and are sensitive to a wide spectrum of color. The center of vision is where precise communication and instruction are received. As you move to the periphery of the retina, rod cells dominate. These are sensitive to faint light and cooler colors and produce less precise, cloudier vision. What has always fascinated us about the eye's sensory ability is that the mechanics do not explain the belief that we inhabit a stable, clear world. There is clearly more at play, of which the eye is but one part. We move our gaze frequently and assemble glances of needed focus, but we are aided by memory, anticipation and, ultimately, a degree of imagination to actively create the appearance of a stable world. Adding the psychological to the visual, Merleau-Ponty posited that humans cannot focus on multiple perspectives at once and that we must push and pull figures in and out of our attention to navigate the world.[10] The world we inhabit at any given moment is, in part, a creative process involving choice and imagination.

In Karl Popper's lecture from 1965, *Of Clocks and Clouds*, he presented a model for thinking about human nature and creative work as an open but softly controlled system.[11] He sees cloud-like systems as more reflective of the dynamic complexity of nature, social systems, and human behavior. By contrast, he proposed that clock-like thinking is the application of objective rational processes and logic. He noted that while objective analysis is important for problem-solving, clock-like thinking by itself does not result in a model of reality that can approach the complex quality of living natural systems. He argued that when a clock-like structure is utilized in isolation, it can be a kind of "deterministic nightmare." Human, social, and institutional systems, like governments, communities, and neighborhoods, can truly be understood and improved if we see them as cloudy clocks.

If design is the design for full-bodied life, then ideas for imagining space have their first presence in the periphery. They are free from the focus of instruction and precedent, as cloud-like structures in the form of a vague description for the feeling of a place. To build the reality promised by these kinds of cloudy ideas, it is necessary to advance the work through its parts in a clock-like way of thinking. This is also the work of imagination—to imagine how each component isolated in the search contributes to a cloudy dynamic space for life. Here, we are reminded of Louis Kahn's declaration that work begins as immeasurable moves through measurable means, and if successful, again becomes immeasurable.[12]

Places are imaginatively inhabited. We employ imagination to anticipate and make engaging space. Today, in the marketplace of architecture and building, there is a lot of pressure for design to predict and measure performance in service of clock-like structures like functional programs, economic proformas, and sustainable and efficiency targets. Attention to these quantifiable systems is important, but for us, architectural design has been a search for an enigmatic, cloudy clock that is socially engaging and culturally meaningful.

45

EXPAND PRACTICE

Why do we use our training on such a small part of the life of a building? Architects are trained to build worlds, full and comprehensive. We acquire the knowledge to conceive of projects, provide innovative designs, and care for buildings to extend their lives. We expand practice to capitalize on the breadth of our knowledge, skill, and potential.

In the first two years of Duvall Decker's existence, we worked out of the second story of our home. Before we had enough work or staff to fill more than 250 square feet, we purchased a 2,900-square-foot building in downtown Jackson with the plan to occupy a portion and lease out the rest. We could barely assemble the cash for the down payment, but we formed a limited liability company and dove in. This was the first of several small real estate purchases and developments that began to teach us about the power of capital investment in buildings to both aid our practice with low overhead and provide long-term investments. We are now working on the fourth building that we plan to occupy. As we moved out of each former building, we leased them to other tenants. Each building provides ongoing positive cash flow and growing equity. As our real estate and financial education progressed, we became skilled at development consulting. On several projects, we secured substantial amounts of capital for our architectural clients. We subdivided this service from the design practice because the valuation of the benefit to the client is very different. We have successfully secured low-income housing tax credits, historic tax credits, municipal and state development incentives, and other negotiated benefits for clients.

After completing our first two K-12 buildings for the Newton Municipal School District, its progressive and dynamic superintendent, Mina Bryan (Bryan-Lightsey), Ph.D., came to trust in our commitment to the district's long-term success. On the one hand, she charged us with planning for the high school campus, and on the other, asked us to help her determine the criteria for hiring custodians and plan for ongoing equipment service and maintenance contracts. We began to learn about the burden of caring for buildings and realized that our knowledge and experience could allow us to provide these services independently of architectural practice.

We now develop projects and provide development consulting through our sister company, Eldon Development, and we provide facilities maintenance through our other sister company, Dunn Management. Duvall Decker provides strategic and community planning services and architectural design. Though the businesses must be distinct, they function as a single studio with everyone learning from the diverse services provided. Duvall Decker creates architecture that is durable in material and memory, cares for buildings to transform daily operation and maintenance into sustained opportunity, and develops with civic-minded innovation to increase the diversity and livability of urban environments.

46

CREATE VALUE

The design of a building is labor-intensive. Design takes time, but the value of the services architects provide, whether innovative thinking, design excellence, or vast experience, is rarely commensurate with the cost to provide those hours of labor. The value created beyond the bounds of standard practice often exceeds the standard compensation. Identify and articulate the value of services, not just their cost.

Architects are hopeful. In the service of design, we see the breadth of opportunity and will labor to do whatever it takes to bring a project to fruition. In a way, this is our professional duty. When we contribute to the health, safety, and welfare of the public, extra time spent is often worth the sacrifice. In our office, we plan our time based on the fee to efficiently complete the work, but at each phase, if the work is not good enough, we look away from the tally of hours and continue until it is. That is the added value we choose to put into the service of our client's mission and the public good.

We are working to measure and communicate the value of design services better. The more we understand the value of good design and identify and distinguish that value for clients, the more design is valued in general. Our efforts take several forms.

For our long-term, non-profit client, Operation Shoestring, we have completed an array of services from facilities maintenance to architectural design and strategic planning over many years. In service of this client's mission and other non-profits, we account for the time and often choose to contribute additional labor beyond the limits of our fixed fees to their capital campaigns.

When we were working with a client to design and build a data center in the historic district of Shreveport, Louisiana, we distinguished the services to document, negotiate, and procure historic tax credits from standard architectural services. We set a separate fee for development consulting as a percentage of the tax credit value for which the owner would receive the benefit.

We completed an assisted living project with fixed architectural fees based on a conservative proforma. This is common and often necessary in the consistently depressed economy of our place. As soon as this project was completed, we watched the rental rates climb immediately and dramatically beyond the proforma and in half of the expected time. Residents and staff reported that they transferred from other facilities to live and work in better-designed spaces. The increased income for the client was a direct result of the quality of the design work. For this increased value created by the quality of the design, we did not receive any additional compensation since we agreed to a fixed fee. We are thrilled for our client and the success of the project, but we do have a hope that design quality in the future will find a voice to be valued on its own terms.

47

IMPACT

Each building/intervention fundamentally changes the experience of a community. Quality should be measured by comprehensive performance. The public impact of the work should expand meaningful social connections, promote mature diversity and density, contribute to community economic growth, and make an ecologically mature and healthy site.

We define comprehensive performance as improvements in social, economic, and environmental systems. We challenge ourselves to improve the health of the environment, identify the social systems that perpetuate inequity and injustice, and in every way that we can, promote a mature society. A mature society would open the center of power to create social, political, and economic opportunities for everyone, particularly those who have long lived in the margins.

All Souls Episcopal Church in Arlington, Texas lost its building after an ideological split in the congregation. After thirteen years in a rented space, the congregation realized that limiting the use of the church building to worship space was an antiquated concept that did not align with their hopes for the future of their church. Congregants also came to see the mission of the church as larger than a denomination. In response to these realizations, the Arlington Center for Community Engagement (ACCE) was created as a secular organization to serve its diverse community. Wellspring on Main, the renovation of a downtown Arlington building, is a development by the ACCE that hopes to remake the nature of religious space to be an open and inviting therapeutic place for the entire community to work together to make a future that is better than the past.

In this work, Duvall Decker serves as both a development consultant and architect. As the development consultant, we support the early process of translating the mission into a program, activities, and services, help find and support the negotiations for a building, and develop financial models to test the planning. ACCE programs and activities that utilize the facility will generate a positive economic impact for the community and ACCE will waive its tax-exempt status to pay a fee in lieu of tax to support city services.

The design for the renovated facility establishes the gathering hall on the ground floor as an invitation and secular sanctuary. A warm, wooden interior hall is visible from the street but veiled by a thin arcade on the outside and a wooden screen inside. The goal is to make a threshold of space that establishes the building as a new form of street-front architecture. This is neither a church set back from the street nor a common commercial storefront building. It is a search to manifest pause, a moment of thin space with a challenge and invitation, a disarming of difference, and an appeal for inquiry. All Souls Episcopal Church will be a tenant in the building and utilize the gathering space for its service on Sunday mornings. Wellspring on Main will be an ecologically mature and healthy structure that will strive to expand meaningful social connections amongst marginalized populations, promote mature diversity, and contribute to the economic growth of its community.

48

MATURE DIVERSITY

Healthy communities and individual growth are best achieved by mature diversity. Dynamic and vibrant communities include people of different races, genders, religions, economic attainment, and educational achievement and provide access to a variety of housing types and sizes, recreation, institutions, services, and jobs.

In his book, *The Uses of Disorder,* Richard Sennett describes the movement towards ordered and specialized communities as one of the great pathological ailments of 20th-century society and its settlements.[13] We first see manifestations of this trend emerge in the early 20th century with the City Beautiful Movement's strategies to make cleaner and healthier cities. After World War II, affluent and middle-class citizens fled cities and often racially diverse communities for more homogeneous, often white, suburbs. Now we see movement to even more elite gated and private neighborhoods.

Homogeneous communities tend to lack the complexity of mature group and individual social relationships. They are often collections of individuals who share an allegiance or identity but do not know each other well. Like-minded individuals living in segregated communities and neighborhoods often avoid exposure to differences and, consequently, develop simplistic moral beliefs about those not like them. Today, as these collections of individuals are exposed to divisive social media and self-selected news, they can grow into tribes. Isolated in space and belief, the opportunities for personal growth that come from the challenges of difference are limited. Society becomes increasingly divided and, in turn, more dysfunctional.

This movement to specialized communities is most harmful when it leaves behind economically and socially starved cities. When businesses and services follow the flight to suburban communities, it starves inner cities of tax revenue. With limited resources for services, deteriorating infrastructure, rising crime, and blight, abandoned inner cities hover near or enter into full crisis. Sennett argues that one therapeutic strategy to mature society and challenge simplistic, moral, tribal divisions may be to radically change our ideas on community planning. He proposes that when individuals are challenged and confronted by difference, possible only when living in diverse urban environments, radical change is possible. The discovery of one's own vulnerability can serve to open empathy for others. He proposes that a functioning city that incorporates the complexity of a healthy "anarchy, diversity, and creative disorder" can foster adults who can openly respond to and better deal with the challenges of life.

Promoting mature diversity is always on our minds as we hope for a healthier community. Whether in a community planning effort, while designing a building floor plan, or bringing the community together to celebrate creative work in our social gatherings or Concrete Studio events, we search for opportunities to make space for diverse meetings. Public cooperation is a learned skill. Architects, buildings, and cities can be teachers and help bring us together. We are often reminded of Michelle Obama's observation, "It's hard to hate up close."[14]

Orchestration

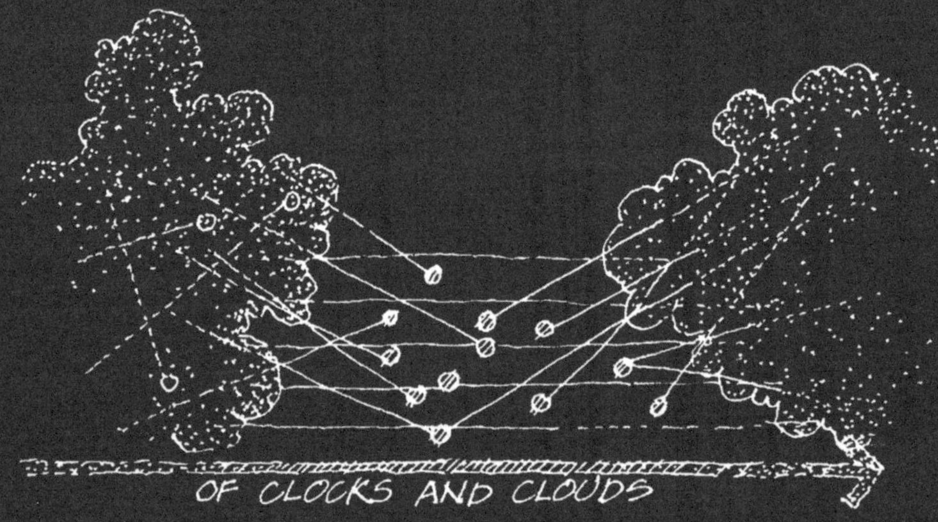

Architects are not like poets, painters, singers, sculptors, or writers—individuals making things they largely control from media they can manipulate directly. Architects are more like composers, directors, or even scientists, sustaining hopeful artistic speculation through conditions, processes, people, and media so broad and distinct as to seem impossible to understand, much less orchestrate.

If one opens to appreciate the distinct character of each of the instruments of an orchestra, the rumbling of a bass drum, the clanging of a cymbal, the trill of a piccolo, the sigh of a violin, the moan of an oboe, the shout of a trumpet, and then listens to a live performance of a symphony, it is miraculous that the character of the music created can have any integrity at all.

For architecture, the distinct influences and players seem ever more diverse and apparently unrelatable. The character of soil varies from soupy sand to destructive expansive clay. The character of place varies from cities built upon thousands of human stories to apparently virgin lands with hidden but compelling histories. The nature of water and moisture changes as it falls upon a surface, drips off of it, travels through it, or glistens upon it. The inescapable pull of gravity exhibits itself differently on each site and inspires varying attitudes of resistance. The play of sunlight transforms from dispersal in the morning fog to highlights and shadows at play on a surface. The character of the wind shifts from wispy nonchalance to violent destruction. The crafts of building evolve from the first moments humans built shelter to their memorializing of people and events in monument. The feats of engineering progress from structure to power, to communication, to mechanics. The intangible potential of shape beckons. The human body and mind viscerally respond to different scales, textures, and characters of space. The capabilities, challenges, and ethics of laborers and craftsmen vary. Clients range from individuals with whims to bureaucracies with missions. The expertise and passions of each person on the project team and the needs and expectations of community members are diverse and distinct. The scope of the capital expenditure can range from limited to vast. The construction process may vary from expedient, to disorganized, to expertly professional.

To orchestrate these broad and distinct players is to invite each wondrous one to influence and support a shared idea, a hopeful and artistic speculation that has the power to build relationships and sustain interest and discipline through the long process of design and building.

After all of it, there are moments when in experiencing our own work, we forget our conceiving of it. Despite all of the words, diagrams, and drawings we used to orchestrate it, words we did not utter in the making inexplicably come forth in attempts to describe it now alive in its place. This is when we hope that we have contributed something to this world that is worth the extensive effort and investment.

49

MEANING

Meaning is pursued, not imposed. Meaning is established first in the architecture of visceral presences, then, on top of this spatial haptic foundation, uses, stories, relations, and connections are layered. Meaning-making is a learned, developed skill.

Meaning is a necessity of human existence. Meaning is not singular nor static; it is alive and in motion. Meaning is not separate from form; it grows from limbic roots up to the surface of language. Inquiry, public communication, and civic debate are skills employed in meaning-making. Without inquiry, there is little possibility for meaning. Without meaning, life becomes a series of disconnected events and reactions to events. John Dewey, in his 1922 essay, "Events and Meanings," notes that if there are only events and no meanings, the world becomes, "dumb, preposterous, even destructive."[15] Neil Postman notes in his book, *Amusing Ourselves to Death*, that a high percentage of the information and events we encounter, often with a propensity for entertainment, has little value in the meaningful decisions we are required to make in our lives.[16] We often find ourselves in the face of an overwhelming storm of entertaining information and disconnected events that dull our sensibilities, undermine our ability for independent thinking, and thwart our efforts to approach the world with skepticism, curiosity, or criticism. We can unwittingly find ourselves consumers and followers under the control of others who perpetuate meaningless events and forms for profit or influence and who ultimately fear change. As we acquiesce, we lose touch with the possibility of a serious, meaningful world and, like Walter Benjamin's angel of history, find ourselves in the face of the storm being blown backward into the future by the detritus of information and events unable to discern a better world.[17]

To consider meaning in architecture is a daunting task. We claim no special theoretical knowledge. Our approach to finding meaningful connections and critiques in form is the result of research, observation, and practice. In the face of the storm, we have practiced acts of critical resistance. We search for the stories suppressed or overlooked. We seek potential connections and relations that coalesce into meaningful interventions. Sometimes it is important to make a restorative proposal. Sometimes it is important to be critical to re-awaken the possibility of inquiry. At Hinds Community College, the Jobie L. Martin Classroom building provides students with a needed gathering space connected to the environment. The north-facing windows diffuse light deep into classrooms and south-facing light lenses track the sun across the sky and down into its public spaces. The spaces are connected to the time of the day, weather, and seasons. The I.T. Montgomery house in Mound Bayou, Mississippi was the home of the founder of one of the first communities in America to be incorporated by formerly enslaved people. Restoration of this home preserves a national treasure and helps tell its story so its significance can be widely shared. In Greenville, Mississippi, a town with a history of sustained inequities, the new U.S. Courthouse relocates the courtrooms, the symbol of power, from deep within the interior of the building out to the street where the promise of access to justice is made visible in a community where it has not always been available.

50

DETAIL

As we get closer to an architecture of quality, it engages us with detail, material life, joinery, ingenuity, and handwork.

The visceral experience of Carlo Scarpa's work elicits a romantic recall of stories of flash-lit evening site visits, hand-drawn construction sketches, and conversations with craftspeople. We might feel nostalgic or even defeated, but we try to adapt.

Like Scarpa, we appreciate the affective potential of materials that are connected directly to the earth and its long history, like the aggregates in concrete, the clay in brick, or the growth rings in wood, and we feel connected to materials that are obviously cut, honed, lifted, laid, or tooled by the human hand.

Unlike Scarpa, we practice in a culture that does not value craft and an economy that cannot support the luxury of idiosyncratic or exploratory detailing. We must detail with the tolerances that allow laborers with limited skills to succeed and the repetition that provides the opportunity to teach craft. The dimensional offset of the blocking from the column grid is explicitly described, but the configuration of the finish anticipates the inaccuracy that is likely to occur. A constructed reveal or a lap of materials assures that a level or plumb line can be struck despite the lack of craft in the substrate. Repetition in the family of detail decisions throughout a project facilitates the craft required for performance while it yields a sense of cohesiveness in the experience of the building.

The design of joints, corners, and edges is informed by the shape and character of the enclosure. Details in masses may be deep and carved. Details in skins may be layered and thin. Whether we are using concrete or brick or the lighter materials often required by tight budgets and expedited schedules, we design surfaces that invite lingering observation and engage environmental phenomena. Too often modern form is conceived from a distance, leaving only vapid surfaces where sealant joints become the only details experienced up close.

We imagine the gravity, thermal movement, rain, and sun acting on the building during construction and over time. We favor architectural dams, channels, and drips over riveted laps and sealant joints. Though we lack the skills to build with our own hands, we can assume the perspective of makers and celebrate hand work. We imagine the order of construction, the size of the crane, lift, or hand that will place materials, the tools that will make the forms or break the metals, or the finishing and cleaning that follows the making.

THE SPRINGDALE MUNICIPAL COMPLEX WAS MADE WITH THE HEADS,
HEARTS, AND HANDS OF MANY INDIVIDUALS. THEY LABORED IN ITS DESIGN AND
CONSTRUCTION AND INVESTED IN ITS MISSION TO SERVE THE CITY OF
SPRINGDALE, ARKANSAS

51

EMBODIED LOYALTY

The site of mature public life is multivalent. In a healthy society, we simultaneously owe loyalties to our most intimate relationships, our partners, family, friends, our neighborhoods, city, and region—as well as our broader allegiances to our country, culture, environment, and species.

In a stable mature society, loyalties grow from the smallest groups, friends, and family to the largest, city, region, country, environment, and species. When threatened from above, small groups contract to protect themselves. The more secure and prosperous a society, the more allegiances grow to larger concerns. When individuals align themselves in tribes based loosely on an appearance of identity, loyalties fracture and become distorted. We all have acquaintances who claim a neighborhood identity but do not know their neighbors, and we have seen inequities in the distribution of resources based on political or racial division.

In a society divided by ideology, class, or race, an individual's moral reasoning can seem superior to others outside their tribe. Agreeable moral principles across the population are less easily understood or applied. The divisive rhetoric that flows from tribal loyalties thwarts our ability for critical and therapeutic conversations about the complex issues that make up our diverse culture and the threats that we face in the environment and as a species. In his lectures on justice, the American pragmatist philosopher, Richard Rorty, makes the case for changing the way we currently rationalize justice. He argues that we should think of justice as "a larger loyalty, to the largest group"—one's fellow citizens, the human species, all living things, and the environment.[18] This changes the focus of moral adjudication from deciding which individual's or tribe's moral reasoning is superior to proposing and describing the conditions of a better way to live.

As architects, we can be agents for more mature conversations in the search for public good. Every project and every meeting can be an opportunity to instigate conversations about our social, environmental, and community health. Architecture for institutions, in our time, should include and prioritize Rorty's call for a "larger loyalty" focus, challenging us to design buildings that participate in and teach us about these shared responsibilities. As we worry about the environment, we must strive to make buildings healthy. As we work to conserve resources, we must design buildings to reduce consumption. As we work to make buildings equitable, we must design buildings to be inclusive. Architecture both records who we are and is a teacher for who we want to become. The embodiment of these larger loyalties into form can help make every design project a teacher.

52

PUBLIC GOOD

Architecture is public work. The horizon of our work is not profit or ego, it is public good.

The search for public good was our earliest foundation, but it was not actually recorded until a few years ago. We added it when we realized it made appearances in other foundations but did not have its own voice on the list. It seemed imperative since most of the lectures we had delivered in the last twenty years were titled "Duvall Decker – Public Work" and the term "public good" was underpinning every project we undertook.

Every project is an opportunity to contribute to the social, environmental, and economic health of a community. Architectural projects can be a force for helping make a better world. But it is important to note that not all projects for public good result in buildings. As a direct result of our focus on public good and our commitment to clients and the communities where we work, we get involved in all types of projects. In Greenville, Mississippi, we helped research and quantify the economic parameters of residents who could not afford the available homes in the market. The Reserves at Gray Park housing project was designed as a middle-city affordable infill housing project to address the economic parameters and this housing gap. For Hope Credit Union, we completed several micro-community planning efforts in towns throughout the Mississippi Delta to support economic mobility for underbanked families. For several years, we have been helping renovate toilets and locker rooms in Jackson Public School buildings. These spaces where young children feel most vulnerable should be clean, bright, safe, and durable. We were also engaged to help the district plan for the reuse of closed schools following its ongoing loss of students and funding over the years. During this work, we discovered that the law that establishes the conditions for the sale of these public properties did not allow housing and mixed-use developments. With the district's support, we wrote a bill to revise the law, and with the help of our state senator and the staff of the lieutenant governor, we successfully lobbied for the changes. The bill, which added housing and mixed-use developments as permissible uses for these closed schools, was passed and signed into law. This change greatly increases the potential for these buildings to be re-developed for uses that will benefit the community and positively impact its economy. For Operation Shoestring, we provided strategic planning support to the board and staff to help focus their services. While we supported the capital campaign that followed the planning, we maintained the failing roof of the existing building to keep it safe and useable until renovations were funded and construction could begin.

For us, design for public good is a prerequisite for design excellence. It is not about appearance or taste nor a question of style. It is not a decorative surplus on top of function or construction. Design excellence for public good is an integral achievement, the result of the search for meaningful form in a particular place that embodies our collective values and human needs and is progressive (a critic and teacher). It is a demonstration of human skill and craft and a commitment to inspiration, education, and grace.

53

BEST IDEA WINS

The best idea wins. Innovative ideas are the most valuable assets a creative organization creates, and as such, Duvall Decker values the voices of all collaborators in the work. Constructive criticisms and suggestions on design solutions, standard practices, daily processes, operations, and quality control are expected and encouraged. While team members may be assigned to one project or work primarily for one company, Duvall Decker recognizes the value of each employee's "roaming rights" to voice their ideas about any project, policy, or company practice. We believe that the quality of the building or environment we are making matters more than any one position, authority, or ego. We value learning from each other and the collaborative practice of recognizing the best ideas from each of us. The best idea wins, every day.

This foundation was written into our office policy in the first few years of the firm. While working on this book, we realized that this fundamental belief, one we repeatedly reference in employee interviews, project interviews, design discussions, community engagement events, pre-construction meetings, and construction site visits, was not on the list. We looked at one another quizzically and added it immediately.

As architects who are trained to envision something that does not exist and pull it into reality, the discipline to listen for and recognize the best idea when it is spoken is an intentional practice and is not always easy. The plan may already meet the complex programmatic area requirements when a flaw in the grace of its procession is identified. The specification for the material may already be written when someone wonders if another material may be more economical or durable. And, hardest, we fall in love with the things we feel we originate. When a better idea is proposed, it is difficult but necessary, in our responsibility to the quality of the work and to empower diverse voices, to embrace the best idea and retrace whatever steps are required to implement it.

Witness

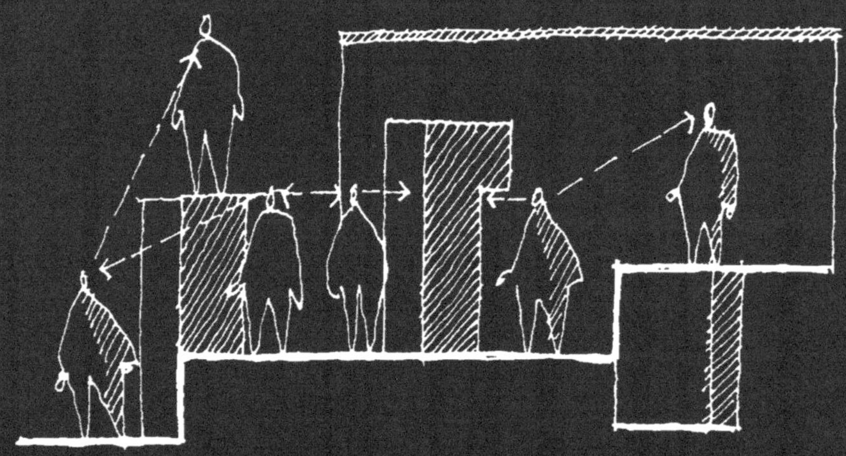

We are each other's witness. We become present in the eyes of others. Our settlements and landscapes are witness to our beliefs and priorities as a culture. Our planet is witness to our consumptive behavior and history of questionable stewardship. We experience spaces as embodied witness. We are not alone; we cannot escape our experience or our relations. We explore, work, play, raise families, negotiate, serve others, all within spaces designed or used for a purpose. Architecture is both a reflection of life and a teacher of a way of living. People are not spectators viewing their world, they are embodied artists and scientists making and exploring their way within a multivalent field filled with complexity and contingencies. As we encounter events, we reflect, compare, analyze, learn, and, in turn, build. Beliefs evolve and are embodied into form. The form of our constructed world is witness to our well-being.

Architects are students of nature and society, its structures, settlements, and landscapes. Architects and designers bear witness to the beauty in humanity, in natural wonders, the structures of settlements, the arts, and all that celebrates humanity's best achievements. Architects also must work to see the unsafe, discriminatory, inhuman, cruel, unjust practices and unhealthy environments.

To practice well is to be honest, humble, responsible, skeptical, critical, and have respect for clients, the public, and the environment. Architects, when we aspire to act as servant leaders and teachers, bear witness to our time and work to create architecture and landscapes that support the pursuit of a future that is better than the past. We fail only when we stop being open to each other with empathy or we deny the responsibility we carry to all others.

In the chapel at Tougaloo College, there is a simple wooden podium. From the podium, many have spoken. During the civil rights movement in the 1960s, the podium supported Martin Luther King Jr., Robert Kennedy, Fannie Lou Hamer, Andrew Young, Medgar Evers, and many others who called for justice, equity, and a future better than the past for all souls in our country. While the work is not done, from this podium the voice of justice was heard, and these voices helped our country mature. The podium's name is Witness.[19]

1. ENIGMA
2. ART
3. ENGAGEMENT
4. CRITICAL PRACTICE
5. ITERATION
6. ETHIC
7. IDEAS
8. CARVED VALUE
9. PRAGMATIC VALUE
10. ECONOMY
11. RESPONSIBILITY
12. RESOLUTE
13. WAKE OF INTEREST
14. DESIGN DEVELOPMENT
15. SCOPE AND DETAIL
16. ACCURACY
17. MANAGEMENT
18. TRUST THE WORK
19. BE FORMAL
20. FEED THE BIRD
21. CRAFTSMANSHIP
22. CHEMISTRY
23. MACHINE
24. TIME
25. COLLABORATE
26. KINSHIP
27. AVOID NOVELTY
28. ORIGINS
29. MOCK IT UP
30. LISTEN BUT LEAD
31. SUCCESS
32. SERVANT LEADER
33. DISCIPLINE
34. RESEARCH
35. INSTITUTIONAL MEMORY
36. ENTANGLEMENT
37. INNOVATION
38. RELEVANCY
39. FORM
40. PUBLIC VALUE
41. COMMUNITY
42. FIRST TEN PERCENT
43. CULTIVATION
44. IMAGINATION
45. EXPAND PRACTICE
46. CREATE VALUE
47. IMPACT
48. MATURE DIVERSITY
49. MEANING
50. DETAIL
51. EMBODIED LOYALTY
52. PUBLIC GOOD
53. BEST IDEA WINS

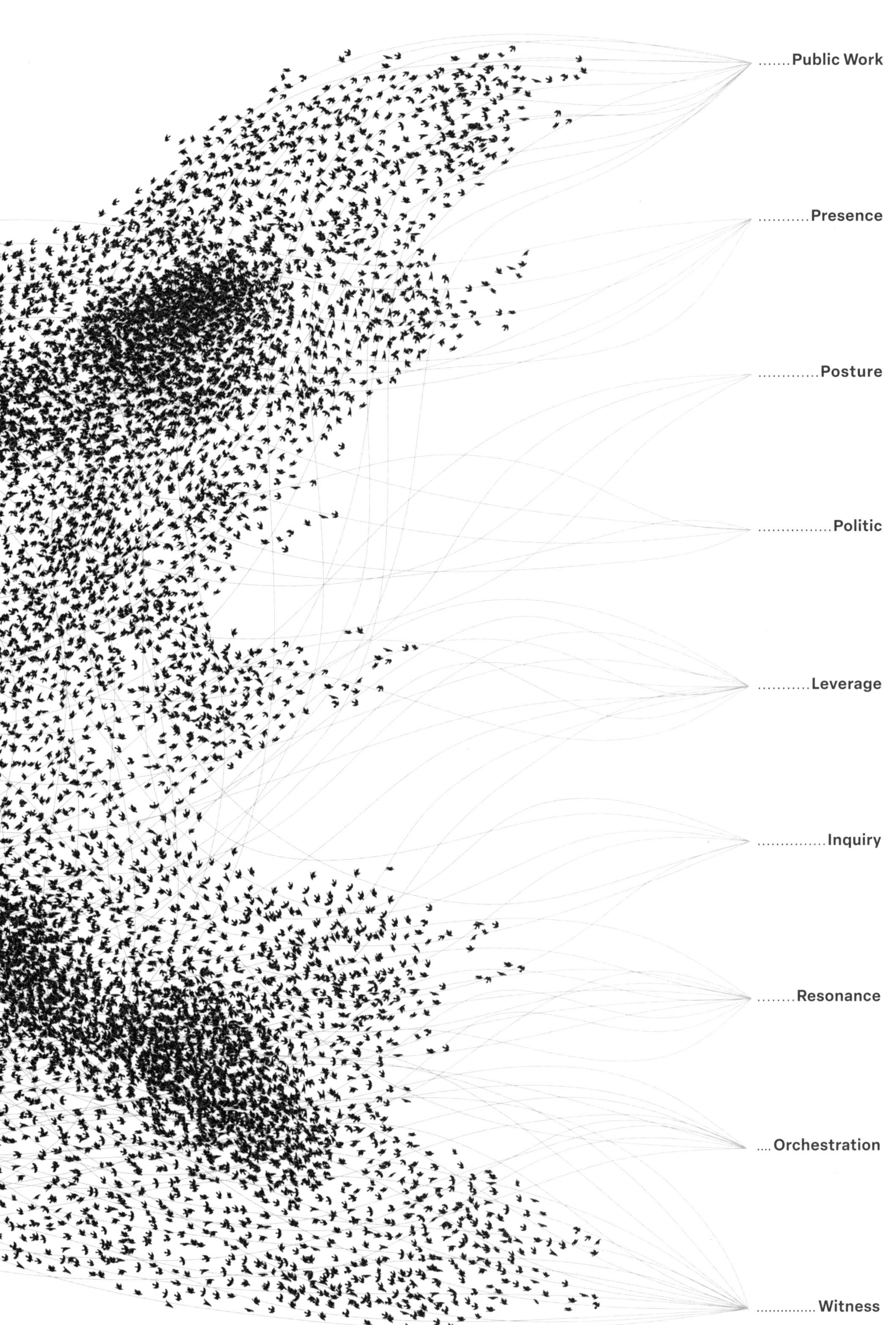

.......Public Work
...........Presence
.............Posture
................Politic
...........Leverage
...............Inquiry
........Resonance
....Orchestration
..............Witness

CONTRIBUTORS

AUTHORS

Anne Marie Duvall Decker, FAIA sees architecture as instrument, engaging the material phenomena of the environment and the culture of place to create work of public value. She leads the studio in creating elusive forms and engaging spaces, no matter the type, size, or budget of projects. Anne Marie is a teacher, design leader, lifelong pianist, and amateur composer.

Anne Marie Duvall Decker received a Bachelor of Architecture degree from Mississippi State University. She is a recognized contributor to the advancement of the profession. She has served as a board member and past President of AIA Mississippi and as a trustee and past Chair of the AIA Trust.

Roy Decker, FAIA expands the role of an architect in the search of public good to include teaching, community organizing, planning, and developing. Roy leads the firm to design public work that is culturally critical, productive, and even therapeutic. Roy is a design and critical thought leader, teacher, and amateur landscape painter.

Roy Decker received a Master of Architecture degree from Kent State University. Prior to the founding of Duvall Decker, he spent over a decade splitting his time between practice and teaching, and he has received recognition and honors for both endeavors.

EDITORS

Jori Erdman, AIA, NOMA
Corrie Kiel
Shannon Gathings, AIA, NOMA
Katherine Flannigan

DESIGN

Katherine Flannigan

COLLABORATORS

Cody Farris, AIA
Shannon Gathings, AIA, NOMA
Krystal Lamm

PHOTOGRAPHY CREDITS

1 SPRINGDALE MUNICIPAL COMPLEX
Duvall Decker | 2022

5 MISSISSIPPI LIBRARY COMMISSION
Timothy Hursley | 2007

7 BENNIE G. THOMPSON ACADEMIC AND CIVIL RIGHTS RESEARCH CENTER
Timothy Hursley | 2012

9 COOPERWOOD SENIOR LIVING
Andrew Welch | 2022

11 MISSISSIPPI LIBRARY COMMISSION
Duvall Decker | 2006

13 MIDTOWN PHASE I
Timothy Hursley | 2012

15 ANG SIMULATION TRAINING FACILITY
Duvall Decker | 2022

17 HARDY MIDDLE SCHOOL, JACKSON PUBLIC SCHOOLS
Duvall Decker | 2018

21 OAK RIDGE HOUSE
Duvall Decker | 2018

23 SELAH HOUSE
Jim Greipp | 2021

25 CANTON READINESS CENTER
Andrew Welch | 2021

27 CANTON READINESS CENTER
Andrew Welch | 2021

29 DUMAS HALL
Timothy Hursley | 2014

31 JAMES H. WHITE LIBRARY
Timothy Hursley | 2015

33 MIDTOWN PHASE 3
Kieth Isaacs | 2017

37 MIDTOWN PHASE 3
Keith Isaacs | 2017

39 DIAZ BOATHOUSE
Duvall Decker | 2003

41 WEST JACKSON MASTER PLAN
Duvall Decker | 2012

43 THE BADDOUR CENTER
Andrew Welch | 2021

45 DUMAS HALL
Duvall Decker | 2014

47 MISSISSIPPI CENTER FOR JUSTICE
Mark Howell | 2013

49 CONSTRUCTION DOCUMENTS
Andrew Welch | 2021

53 OAK RIDGE HOUSE
Timothy Hursley | 2012

55 MISSISSIPPI LIBRARY COMMISSION
Timothy Hursley | 2007

57 BENNIE G. THOMPSON ACADEMIC AND CIVIL RIGHTS RESEARCH CENTER
Duvall Decker | 2010

59 SPRINGDALE MUNICIPAL COMPLEX
Duvall Decker | 2022

61 THE RESERVES AT GRAY PARK
Andrew Welch | 2021

63 WIGGS POOLHOUSE
Timothy Hursley | 2016

65 YELVERTON LAKE HOUSE
Duvall Decker | 2002

69 MENDENHALL ELEMENTARY
Eric Hudson | 2007

71 TEAM
Duvall Decker, 2022

73 MIDTOWN PLANNING
Kieth Isaacs | 2017

75 COOPERWOOD SENIOR LIVING
Andrew Welch | 2022

77 BENNIE G. THOMPSON ACADEMIC AND CIVIL RIGHTS RESEARCH CENTER
Timothy Hursley | 2012

79 U.S. COURTHOUSE GREENVILLE MOCK UP
Duvall Decker, 2020

81 THE BADDOUR CENTER
Andrew Welch | 2021

85 OAK RIDGE HOUSE
Timothy Hursley | 2012

87 OPERATION SHOESTRING
Andrew Welch, 2022

89 BENNIE G. THOMPSON ACADEMIC AND CIVIL RIGHTS RESEARCH CENTER
Timothy Hursley | 2012

91 MENDENHALL GYM
Eric Hudson, 2006

93 MATERIALS, SPRINGDALE MUNICIPAL COMPLEX
Duvall Decker, 2022

95 JOBIE L. MARTIN CLASSROOM BUILDING
Mark Howell | 2012

97 MISSISSIPPI LIBRARY COMMISSION
Timothy Hursley | 2007

101 COOPERWOOD SENIOR LIVING
Andrew Welch | 2022

103 JOBIE L. MARTIN CLASSROOM BUILDING
Mark Howell | 2012

105 MS DEPT. OF INFORMATION TECHNOLOGY SERVICES AGENCY DATA CENTER
Timothy Hursley | 2015

107 MS DEPT. OF INFORMATION TECHNOLOGY SERVICES AGENCY DATA CENTER
Timothy Hursley | 2015

109 COAHOMA COUNTY HIGHER EDUCATION CENTER
James Patterson | 2011

111 MIDTOWN PHASE 3
Kieth Isaacs | 2017

113 NEWTON HIGH SCHOOL
Duvall Decker | 2004

117 MISSISSIPPI LIBRARY COMMISSION
Timothy Hursley | 2007

119 MISSISSIPPI LIBRARY COMMISSION
Timothy Hursley | 2007

121 MIDTOWN PHASE 2
Kieth Isaacs | 2017

123 JAMES H. WHITE LIBRARY
Timothy Hursley | 2015

125 OPERATION SHOESTRING
Andrew Welch | 2020

127 COOPERWOOD SENIOR LIVING
Andrew Welch | 2022

129 WEST MILLSAPS HOUSING
Kieth Isaacs | 2017

133 SELAH HOUSE
Jim Greipp | 2021

135 SPRINGDALE MUNICIPAL COMPLEX
Duvall Decker | 2023

137 SELAH HOUSE
Jim Greipp | 2021

139 SPRINGDALE MUNICIPAL COMPLEX
John Melendez | 2023

141 U.S. COURTHOUSE GREENVILLE
Duvall Decker | 2023

143 DUVALL DECKER STUDIO
Duvall Decker | 2007

147 THE BADDOUR CENTER
Andrew Welch | 2021

153 ANNE MARIE & ROY
Kieth Isaacs | 2021

DEDICATION

We dedicate this work of our search for art and public good to those we have learned from, those who have inspired us, those who have been influential in our lives, those whom we serve, and our families.

Walter Warmath, Brian Coopersmith, David Cronrath, Osyp Martyniuk, Jack Kremers, Hunter Morrison, Michael Fazio, Chris Risher, Jr., Michael Mitias, Eudora Welty, Frank Figgers, Bill Easom, Sharman Smith, Mina Bryan, Sheila Jackson, Beverly Wade Hogan, Congressman Bennie Thompson, Col. Paul McDonald, Daniel Boggs, Parke Pepper, David Reyff, Kelle Menogan, Carmen Walters, Graham Ashmead, Walt Cabe, Medgar Evers, Adrian Stokes, Melanie Klein, Richard Sennett, John Dewey, Richard Rorty, Elaine Scarry, Umberto Eco, Atul Gawande, Edgar Allan Poe, Neil Postman, Ludwig Wittgenstein, Maurice Merleau-Ponty, Daniel Kahneman, bell hooks, Paul Cezanne, Martin Puryear, Robert Irwin, Alberto Giacometti, Johannes Vermeer, Constantin Brancusi, Richard Kelso, Claude Debussy, Hector Villa Lobos, Eric Satie, Max Richter, Peter Gabriel, Paul Simon, The National, Christopher Nolan, Denis Villeneuve, Alvar Aalto, Aldo van Eyck, Le Corbusier, Marlon Blackwell, Ati Blackwell, Tod Williams, Billie Tsien, Paul Mankins, Steve Dumez, Michael LeBoeuf, Derrick Johnson, Letitia Johnson, Eric Green, Jori Erdman, George Dodds, Cody Farris, Shannon Gathings, Krystal Lamm, Carol Decker, Roy E. Decker, Clint Decker, Pauline Brown, Jane Duvall, Robert L. Duvall, Michelle Blanton, Tracy Hamm, Evan Duvall Decker, Avery Anne Decker.

DUVALL DECKER

Duvall Decker Architects was founded in 1998 in Jackson, Mississippi. The firm is an expanded practice whose work includes architectural design, community planning, real estate development, and facility maintenance. Duvall Decker designs, plans, develops, and cares for built environments to leverage the best of human endeavors and foster education, cultural growth, and environmental health. The firm is dedicated to the creation of forms and environments that enrich the lives of those who encounter and inhabit them.

Duvall Decker has been honored with many peer-reviewed design awards and has been selected for national design excellence projects such as the new Federal Courthouse in Greenville, Mississippi (a GSA Design Excellence project) and the new Springdale, Arkansas Municipal Complex (a Walton Family Foundation Design Excellence project). The firm's work and approach have been highlighted in publications such as *The New York Times*, *dwell*, *ARCHITECT* Magazine, *Architectural Record*, *The Journal of Architectural Education*, and the *Oxford American*. In 2017, the Architectural League of New York selected Duvall Decker as one of its Emerging Voices, and in 2019, the firm was highlighted as a "Game Changer" by *Metropolis*. In 2023, Anne Marie Duvall Decker was a recipient of *Architectural Record's* Women in Architecture Design Leadership Award. *The Architect's Newspaper* named the firm the Best Medium Firm in the Southeast as part of its Best in Practice Awards.

PAST AND CURRENT ASSOCIATES

Rachel Acord, Vivian Adams, Charles Alexander, Cindi Alexander, David Alvarez Cobo, Roderick Austin, **Torrie Austin,** Emily Baker, **Olivia Baker, Daniel Barker,** Stacy Banks, Audrey Bardwell, Anna Kathryn Becker, Samantha Blanton, **Katie Bowen,** Trey Box, **Tommy Boykin,** Amy Bridge, Michael Brown, **Stephene Butler,** Daniel Burks, Matthew Cadle, Amanda Campbell, Jordan Carter, Nkosazana Cetewayo, Elizabeth Cockrell, Alison Cunningham, Brett Cupples, Christopher Davis, Michael Davis, **Tim Dean, Anne Marie Duvall Decker,** Avery Decker, Evan Decker, **Roy Decker,** Bustillo Dilcia, LaToya Dixon, William Doran, Karen Dudley, Robert Farr, Elizabeth Farrell, **Cody Farris, Katherine Flannigan, Shannon Gathings,** Danielle Glass, Steve Green, Ryan Hansen, Molly Hartzog, Latasha Hatten, Meredith Head, Holly Hearon, Zachary Henry, Cailin Herring, Betsy Hewett, **Madison Holbrook,** Melanie Holmes, Carolyn Hudson, Jennifer Jackson, Patrick Jackson, Kevin Jeffers, Brad Jeffries, Allison Jenkins, Gloria Jimerson, **Corrie Kiel,** Marlan Kyles, **Krystal Lamm,** Anastasia Lawson, Lynn Leach, Jonathan LeJune, **Mila Lipinski**, Mitchell Lloyd, Qubert Maxie, Dennis McGee, Courtney McLaurin, Melody Moody, **Hattie Morrison,** Chris Myers, Joseph Nelson, Alex Nevarez, Ortiz Todd, Nichols Ja'tel Norals, Karissa Norwood, Jesse O'Quinn, Mary Osborne, **Chris Osterlund,** Sarah Page, Prem Patel, Linda Perkes, Matthew Persinger, Jocelyn Poe, Joshua Reeder, **Sheri Ross,** Dawn Rueff, John Schaffhauser, Laken Sells, Bonnie Shetler, Andrea Simms, Daniel Smith, Kemper Smith, Shayla Smith, Irma Stewart, Alissa Tang, Matthew Thompson, **Larry Flowers**, Austin Turcotte, Tony Vance, Gabriel Vandegrift, Kristen Vise, Elizabeth Waits, Cheryl Walton, Irma Ward, Newell Watkins, Leah Welborn, Jeremy West, Kyle Wherry, Antonia Wickersham, Nicholas Wickersham, Christina Wilburn, Heather Wilcox, Richard Williams, Kenetra Willams, Victoria Wolfe, Edwin Woolfolk, Laquita Wright, Terrance Yates

REFERENCE

1 Kenneth Frampton, "Towards a Critical Regionalism: Six Points for an Architecture of Resistance" *The Anti-Aesthetic: Essays on Postmodern Culture* (Michigan: Bay Press, 1983), 14.

2 John Dewey, *Experience and Nature* (New York: Dover Publications, 2000), 24.

3 Adrian Stokes, *The Image in Form, Selected Writings of Adrian Stokes*, ed. Richard Wollheim (New York: Harper & Row, 1972), 26.

4 Atul Gawande, *The Checklist Manifesto* (London: Picador, 2011), 46.

5 Richard Sennett, *The Craftsman* (New Haven: Yale University Press, 2009), 60.

6 Lawrence Wheschler, *Seeing is Forgetting the Name of the Thing One Sees* (Oakland: University of California Press, 2009), 76.

7 bell hooks, "Choosing The Margin as A Space of Radical Openness," *Framework: The Journal of Cinema and Media*, no. 36 (Michigan: Wayne State University Press, 1989), 78.

8 Erik Satie, *Pieces Froides (Reinbert De Leeuw)* (Australia: Brolga Music Publishing Company, 1897), 98.

9 Daniel Patrick Moynihan, Guiding Principles for Federal Architecture. Ad Hoc Committee on Federal Office Space, 1962. 104.

10 Merleau-Ponty, *Phenomenology of Perception*, trans. Donald Landes (Abingdon: Routledge, 2013), 122.

11 Karl Popper, *Of Clocks and Clouds: An Approach to the problem of rationality and the freedom of man* (St. Louis, Washington University, 1996), 122.

12 Louis Kahn and John Lobell, *Between Silence and Light: Spirit in the Architecture of Louis I. Kahn* (Boulder: Shambhala Publications, 2008), 122.

13 Richard Sennet, *Uses of Disorder: Personal Identity and City Life* (New York: W. W. Norton & Company, 1992), 130.

14 Michelle Obama, *Becoming* (New York: Crown, 2018), 130.

15 John Dewey, "Events and Meanings" *Essays on Philosophy, Education, and the Orient*, vol. 13 (Illinois: Southern Illinois University Press, 1922), 136.

16 Neil Postman, *Amusing Ourselves to Death: Public Discourse in the Age of Show Business* (New York: Penguin Books, 2005), 136.

17 Walter Benjamin, *Illuminations*, ed. Hannah Arendt, trans. Harry Zohn (New York: Schocken Books, 1969), 136.

18 Richard Rorty, *Philosophy as Cultural Politics, Philosophical Papers*, Vol 4. (Cambridge: Cambridge University, 2007), 140.

19 Mad Genius, "Silent Witness Poem", 2019, 146.

Publishers of Architecture, Art, and Design
Gordon Goff: Publisher

www.oroeditions.com
info@oroeditions.com

Published by ORO Editions

Graphic Design: Katherine Flannigan
Text: Anne Marie Duvall Decker, FAIA; Roy Decker, FAIA
ORO Managing Editor: Kirby Anderson

10 9 8 7 6 5 4 3 2 1 First Edition

Library of Congress data available upon request. World Rights: Available

ISBN: 978-1-957183-51-0

Color Separations and Printing:
ORO Editions, Inc.
Printed in China.

International Distribution:
www.oroeditions.com/distribution

ORO Editions makes a continuous effort to minimize the overall carbon footprint of its publications. As part of this goal, ORO Editions, in association with Global ReLeaf, arranges to plant trees to replace those used in the manufacturing of the paper produced for its books. Global ReLeaf is an international campaign run by American Forests, one of the world's oldest nonprofit conservation organizations. Global ReLeaf is American Forests' education and action program that helps individuals, organizations, agencies, and corporations improve the local and global environment by planting and caring for trees.

This is one studio's search for public good.

FOUNDATIONS